Praise for the authors of
Fuel an Extraordinary Life…

"Throughout his long career Dick Rogala skillfully guided people along the pathways of self-awareness critical to leading a successful life. As a mentor, he has enriched my life personally and professionally. His insights are timeless."

Frank LaFasto, Ph.D.
Senior Vice President
Cardinal Health

"Dick Rogala's incisive analyses lead to my broader understanding of critical issues and provided guidance towards proper action in business situations. A keen student of leadership and motivation, Dick was always able to help me work through the challenges of achieving life goals. 'Face the issue' was an early lesson that still provides direction."

Bill Gardner
Distribution Properties LLC

"Dick and his son Rick have the remarkable ability to view every situation with the wise combination of an infectious positive spirit, a rock solid belief in people, and the importance of authenticity in every thing you do. They have the ability to coach others to a higher level of performance with a contagious enthusiasm based upon seeing 'every glass as half full rather than half empty' and a 'focused simplicity' of a rifle shot. Everyone can experience higher levels of success with exposure to these remarkable individuals."

Doug Park
President
SWCC Inc.

"My time with Rick Rogala was some of the most rewarding years of my career. His unique style of leadership inspired me and the rest of the team to work in an empowered manner to set difficult goals and achieve them. I continue to put things I learned from Rick to work for me and my company every day."

Dan Bradley
Vice President of News
Media General Broadcast Group

"Rick is a natural leader of men and woman who engages people around him. His energetic, insightful approach is refreshing in today's supremely competitive business environment. I've worked with, for, and against him; they don't come any brighter."

Mike Hayes
President and General Manager
WYFF-TV

Who Can Benefit from Reading this Book?	Who Won't Benefit from Reading this Book?
Nurse	A person with a closed mind
Salesperson	A person who does not care to learn
Minister	A person who does not care to improve
Grandparent	
Engineer	
Entrepreneur	
Anyone who has read Jim Collins brilliant book *Good to Great* and would like to be "the right person on the bus."	
Teacher	
Student	
Manager	
Small Business Owner	
Installer	
Technician	
Mechanic	
Parent	
Executive Assistant	
Marketing Executive	
Fan of Stephen Covey	
Coach	
Graphic Designer	
Computer Programmer	
Government Employees	
CEO	
Accountant	
Journalist	
Maintenance Worker	
Landscaper	
Dreamer	
Teenager	
Scientist	
Welder	
Chef	
Person searching for their first job	
Retiree	
Cosmetologist	
Realtor	
Fire Fighter	
Actor	
Cashier	

Fuel an Extraordinary Life!

By

Richard E. Rogala Ph.D.
And
Richard E. Rogala, Jr.

authorHOUSE™

1663 LIBERTY DRIVE, SUITE 200
BLOOMINGTON, INDIANA 47403
(800) 839-8640
WWW.AUTHORHOUSE.COM

First published by AuthorHouse 01/04/05

ISBN: 1-4208-1153-3 (e)
ISBN: 1-4208-1154-1 (sc)
ISBN: 1-4208-2038-9 (dj)

Library of Congress Control Number: 2004098869

Printed in the United States of America
Bloomington, Indiana

This book is printed on acid-free paper.

"The most lasting gift that you can give your children is your time. It's the gift that will make them the happiest and will leave them with that solid feeling that they are worth your time."

Dad... you are my hero.
I love you.

Table of Contents

Foreword

Thank you for making an investment and buying this book. It is an investment of your money and an investment of your time. In today's world, there is nothing more valuable.

In buying this book, it could be that you are searching for answers to questions that you have about achieving your goals, or you could be looking for information about how others have achieved success. You may be looking to learn more about yourself. Like so many of us, you may be trying to find ways to jumpstart a weight loss program or improve a relationship. Maybe you are looking for ways to grow your business, or take that next step in your career. You may even be looking for ways to create wealth. And just maybe, you are looking to create a richness of life beyond your wildest imagination. There are answers in this book, guideposts to living a wonderful life and achieving your dreams.

This is not a quick fix book.

Ask anyone who has read the latest fad book more than six months ago to describe the specifics offered as solutions to problems. The likelihood is that they will mumble some quick generalizations, if they are able to remember anything at all. Often, however, they will simply say that the book was great. The improvement described in this book requires effort and practice. Unlike a quick fix, it is the type of improvement that can last a lifetime.

When put into place, the attributes we outline will help lead you on the path from ordinary to extraordinary. Harnessed with values like integrity, honesty and kindness, these attributes will help you to achieve your dreams and live a wonderful life. A wise person once said "If we always do what we've always done, we won't always get what we've always had. We will get less." In other words, stand still and you will actually move backward. The development of these attributes will help you make the forward progress you deserve.

Our goal is not to define your vision of a wonderful life. That vision rests with you. We want to provide an outline of the tools necessary to make your vision a reality.

We want to help you to live a wonderful, extraordinary life.

You can do it!

Part I
Inspiration

Chapter 1

The Hero

"I studied the lives of great men and famous women, and I found that the men and women who got to the top were those who did the jobs they had in hand, with everything they had of energy and enthusiasm and hard work."
-Harry S. Truman

The most precious resource on earth is not oil, electricity, water, air or mineral; it is the power and energy of the human spirit.

Because of the capability and strength of the human spirit, men and women have the capacity to dream and imagine, to create and accomplish the extraordinary. It has the power to fuel positive change in our lives and allows for the curing of disease, the creation of art, and the advancements of technology and society. The potential of the human spirit is limitless.

The human spirit is also the most underutilized resource on earth. Even with the power and resource available to us, famine, war, disease and other terrible problems still permeate our world.

Hope springs from the capacity that each of us has to harness the power of our human spirit. It resides within us, waiting to be unleashed. We alone control the decision to let loose its potential and move from ordinary to the extraordinary. No one can ever take that away.

An extraordinary life is well within your reach and the path is clearly marked.

This is a roadmap for success based on sixty years of combined experience in business and over one hundred combined years of living life enthusiastically and passionately. It is based on observing, listening to and learning from some of the most talented people in business and education. These are guideposts based on tremendous personal success, and the heart wrenching failures that come with risk. Most importantly, it is a roadmap based on the teachings of a very wise and successful man who lived an extraordinary, wonderful life.

Fatherly Inspiration

Looking back, I realized at a fairly young age that my father was a special man. He made me laugh. He was kind, gentle and strict, all at the same time. Like many fathers, he threw the football around; he played catch with the baseball and played basketball in the back yard. He always showed an interest in my sister and me and the things that we cared about. And, despite working exhaustive hours and traveling constantly, he always seemed to show up at the events that are important to you as a kid: a football game, the science fair, a spring sing, and a band concert.

His arrival at events was always greatly anticipated. Would his plane be on time? Would there be traffic? Would some type of delay keep him from listening to this once-in-a-lifetime event of a group of second graders singing about the adventures of Johnny Appleseed?

The lights are dim. The over anxious music teacher is seen standing before the group of fidgeting eight-year-old future virtuosos. And, just as the pitch pipe is raised to the lips for that first note, the door to the back of the gym opens. The light from the hallway behind the door splashes around the shadow of a tall, muscular figure slipping into the gym, just in time. Dad's here. Life is good. All is safe in the world.

Despite the often last-minute entrances that would seemingly shed attention to his presence, Dad shunned the limelight. At baseball games he would favor standing behind the right field fence to watch the game rather than sitting in the stands. He said that it gave him a chance to really enjoy watching his children, to savor the moments that came with each triumph, and to sympathize with the heartache of each failure.

Whether playing first base, catching a pass, or making a lay-up, it never bothered me that I could always hear my friends' dads in the stands. It never bothered me because I could *feel* my Dad's presence and I knew that with one quick turn of the head, I would see his smile and his thumb's up. I knew he loved me, whether I caught the pass or struck out with the bases loaded.

It wasn't until later in life, as I reached adulthood, that I realized my father was much more than special. He was extraordinary.

An Extraordinary Life

Richard E. Rogala's life began on the west side of Chicago in a working class Polish neighborhood. The stories of his youth are mixed with joy and pain. The stories of joy were told by him: his love for his brother and sister, his grandmother, and his Uncle Eddy. The stories of pain we learned later in life from my mother and other relatives: stories about having to throw a shoe up the back porch to scatter the rats when coming home from work as a teenager, of being sent to the coal storage basement, fighting off the rats, and shoveling coal for the only heat in the house, and other stories, that he would not want repeated.

His family did not have money, so he worked to put himself through St. Mel's High School. He passed on the opportunity to play football and basketball for St. Mel, sports he loved, in order to work and help support his family. During the summers he worked for a Catholic settlement house, Marillac House in Chicago, and acted as a camp counselor to inner city kids. It was there he met the two greatest influences in his life-- his future wife and a nun named Sister Mary William, who ran the settlement house. With the love and support of his wife to be and Sister Mary William, Dad pursued his dream of going to college. He entered DePaul University on a Drama scholarship, but quickly fell in love with the discipline of psychology. Psychology and his family became his passions.

Dad and Mom were married at the young ages of 22 and 20 respectively. They started a family, and Dad pursued his dream of becoming a psychologist. He received his Masters in Psychology from DePaul University, and went on to work on his PhD in clinical psychology. During that time, he supported a family, studied full time for his doctorate, and worked three jobs at one time: teaching at Lewis University and working with St. Joseph's Carondelet Child Center and Angel Guardian Orphanage.

As a young boy I saw my father awarded his doctorate in clinical psychology from the Illinois Institute of Technology in a dark, noisy, hot gym, with a Chicago elevated train interrupting the ceremony from time to time. I remember that day vividly, not because I understood the significance of the sacrifices that my parents had made or all of the hard work that my father had put forth, but because of the smile on his face and the gleam in his eye. It was the face of joy and accomplishment.

He continued to work for Lewis University, serving as chairman of the psychology department, and subsequently was named Director of Institutional Research and Assistant to the President of the University. Not long after, he was recruited into the private sector.

He worked for eighteen years with a firm of psychologists as a consultant to management, working with some of the finest and most prestigious companies in America. The last five of those eighteen years he served as president of the organization. And then, my father did something that so many people dream about but never get to do in their lifetime: he went out on his own.

Dad started his own firm in 1986. Based upon his reputation and work ethic, he quickly built the firm Rogala and Associates into one of top management consulting firms in the U.S. His work conducting management assessments, coaching and counseling executives and managers, utilizing group techniques to help develop managers and team building made him one of the most sought after teachers in the country. And yet, in talking with him, you would never know any of this. Through his success, he remained humble. And, what he really enjoyed talking about, what he found great joy in, was the success and life experiences of others.

The majority of his life was spent helping others: listening, teaching, providing for their well-being and leading by example. He helped people in profound ways, and he helped people in simple ways. He loved to learn from others and share what he learned. He loved to help people achieve their dreams. He was a remarkable teacher and an extraordinary man.

Lessons of a Father

So much of what I learned in life, I learned from my Dad. To some, I was a sweaty, overactive, talkative (okay, way too talkative) little boy. Apparently, the words listen, sit down, and walk were not in my vocabulary. And, after seeing home movies of myself over and over, I really couldn't argue the point. Back then, I was annoying. In today's world, I'd probably be medicated. Thank goodness Dad and Mom saw other things. Dad taught me to listen. He taught me the value of learning, of questioning and of wonder. He taught me to focus, and to harness my energy. He taught me the importance of laughter, especially at oneself.

As I entered my professional life as a broadcaster and followed my own dreams, I found myself constantly calling on lessons that my dad had taught me. Some of those lessons came from stories that he told of people that he had met in his work, and of their accomplishments and growth (he never used names; that was always kept confidential). Other lessons came from watching him interact with people and counsel friends of mine who would seek his opinion. Still other lessons came as I brought him problems, predicaments and issues from my own professional and personal life. After listening intently and asking questions, his counsel would always begin the same way: "What do you think you should do?" To a teenager, this was maddening. To a young professional, it was eye opening and inspiring. As his student, it was brilliant.

What my dad taught me is that there is a core set of attributes that people possess who love their lives, achieve their goals, fulfill their dreams and live wonderful lives. The happiest people I have ever known possess these attributes. The most consistently successful people I have ever known possess these attributes. Organizations that achieve great things are typically made up of people who share these attributes. What my dad taught me was reinforced again and again as I learned from others and observed people in my professional life.

As I applied what my dad taught me, I was able to achieve things that I dreamed about, and some things I never dreamed possible: first place in a State Science Fair, National Honor Societies, first place in speech competitions, college scholarships and awards, being the youngest person hired for an advanced training program, becoming the president of a business unit in my early thirties, building three television stations, two from the ground up, and leading teams and organizations to extraordinary growth.

Best of all, I was able to watch people around me, the people that I work with, live with and play with, achieve extraordinary things in their lives and teach me lessons on a daily basis. All of these people who were experiencing incredible achievements and living wonderful lives share those same basic attributes that Dad taught to me.

The Greatest Lessons

Probably the most significant lessons that my Dad taught me were during the last ten years of his life. Two years after having started his own firm, at the age of 52, Dad was diagnosed with lung cancer. He had been a smoker since he was a teenager, when smoking was cool. As time went on, and he knew he had to quit, he moved to small cigars and then to a pipe.

Finally, with the strength of character that he demonstrated throughout his life, he quit cold turkey. Ten years later, on a fall afternoon, he was given the news that no one ever wants to hear.

The news was not good. The initial prognosis did not give him much of a chance to live for more than a year. The plan of action called for surgery to remove a section of lung and chemotherapy. Dad always believed in seeking wise counsel and putting faith in those people, so he sought out the best oncologist and surgeon. They told him that while surgery and drugs were important, the critical piece of the formula would be his attitude. The ministers were preaching to the choir.

What followed was an amazing journey of courage, faith, the power of positive thinking and love. With the help of my Mom, an amazing woman in her own right, Dad not only survived his first battle with cancer, but he was able to recover and continue to build his firm. A few years later, after a brain tumor was found, he once again approached his battle with the same courage and positive attitude as before. And again, he recovered and continued to build his business.

After ten years of fighting and laughing and building and continuing to live a wonderful life, lung cancer was discovered once again.

During those ten years, despite the odds, despite illness and despite the harsh effects of treatment, Dad lived with gusto and passion. He got to know his grandchildren and they got to know and love their Poppy. He taught them lessons that to this day they remember and hold close. He traveled and he worked and he continued on his journey of learning, teaching and helping people achieve their dreams.

He never gave up. In his final days, surrounded by his family, his body finally failing him, he still was able to smile, and with a twinkle in his eye, let you know that he loved you. He didn't talk about dying. He talked about angels, and his wonderful doctors, his grandchildren and his family. And then, the man who loved life with abandon, lived to help other people and believed in living each day to its fullest, slipped away.

Dad and I had talked about writing a book together. He had published many, many articles as a management consultant all geared toward helping people become better managers, listeners, and team members. We talked about how much we had learned from our failures and successes, how much we had learned from the wise people that we had worked for, and the painful lessons that we learned from the evil people with whom we worked. We had discussed writing a book about the core attributes of people who live wonderful lives, but the joy of living and his courageous battle took precedence.

This book is based on Dad's writings and teachings. He is my co-author, my inspiration and my hero. It's based on the heart-wrenching failures and joyful success that we have lived and experienced. And, it is based on our time with those incredible people who have inspired us, motivated us, and taught us so much about living life, dreaming dreams, success and achievement.

What is an extraordinary life? What do we mean by achieving dreams? Simply put, an extraordinary life is a life full of joy, satisfaction, positive challenge and happiness. It's waking up each day excited about what life has in store. It's going to bed each evening pleased with the piece of life you have lived and wanting to do it all over again the next day.

Living an extraordinary life is about learning and continually growing, in the company of people who love you. It's about setting goals, and achieving those goals. It's about making a real difference in other people's lives and making their lives extraordinary. It is leading by example, and following with courage.

The terrific thing is that *you* set the parameters for your extraordinary life and the dreams you want to achieve. Do you want to lose weight? Do you want to finish your education? Do you want to improve a relationship that is failing? Do you want to earn a fortune? Do you want to own your own business? Do you want to be recognized as the best salesperson in your company?

Read, learn, practice… and you will live an extraordinary life and achieve your dreams.

Part II
The Eight Attributes that Fuel an Extraordinary Life!

Chapter 2

You Can Do It!

"Decision and determination are the engineer and fireman of our train to opportunity and success."
-Burt Lawlor

As a teenager, we long for the days when we can make our own decisions and get out from underneath our parents' rules. Then as we mature, it seems the more responsibilities we have, the more we yearn for the days when the most we had to worry about was whether there would be a swing open on the playground during recess. However, the days that we should really yearn for are the days that we can't even remember. It was the golden first six first months of life. Eat, sleep, and poop. Dream a little bit, wake up, people smile at you, kiss you, feed you and put you back to sleep. Dream a little bit more. And here's the best part. If we cried, or had some gas, or our older sibling pinched us, we can't even remember. Ah, the good life.

Decisions, Decisions

Next stage: we are thrust into a world of decision-making. It starts fairly simply. Would we like peaches or pears? Chocolate or strawberry? Do you want to wear the blue shirt, or the red shirt? And then suddenly, the decisions become more complex. Should I cross the street? Should I climb on that counter? If I tease my sister will Dad really pull the car over? As a teenager or an adult, we wish the decisions we are faced with every day were that simple. In today's complicated world, we are faced every day with intricate problems requiring decisions that affect our jobs, our relationships, our health and in some cases, the rest of our lives.

With as many decisions as we need to make throughout our lives, and as early in life as we begin to make decisions, you would think that decision-making would be something that would come easy to just about everyone. And yet, so many of us are paralyzed when it comes time to make a decision. We hem, we haw, we think, we over think, we procrastinate, and many times we hope that someone else will make a decision for us, or that by not making a decision, the problem will go away.

Regardless of the reason, not making a decision most often ends up with a lack of action or forward progress on our part. And any time we aren't moving forward, with as fast as the world moves and changes around us, it's guaranteed you're not standing still; you're moving backward. This book is definitely *not* about moving backward.

Time to Take Action

A terrific lesson in decision making and the importance of belief came to us in the mid-70's by way of a Catholic priest who was serving at St. Louise de Marillac Parish in suburban Chicago. His name was Father John R. Keating, and he was a cannon lawyer for the archdiocese of Chicago. He would say Mass and serve the Parish, and also served as vicar general and chancellor of the Chicago archdiocese.

One particular warm Sunday morning Father Keating was presiding over a Mass which our whole family was attending. The Mass had proceeded as usual, the Gospel had been read, and we were settling into our seats for the homily (sermon).

As a teenager, one worked hard to understand the message of the homily. One worked hard to pay attention. One tried not to let one's mind drift to thoughts of activities planned for later that afternoon, to a game next weekend, or to that place of empty space that teenage minds so often travel. As an adult and parent, one worked hard to nudge the teenager back into reality, and to give the appropriate look that meant: "Pay attention. Important Message Ahead."

None of these events occurred this Sunday morning. Father began speaking, and every eye was on him. His voice carried a message of inspiration unlike any we had heard. His quiet demeanor and enthusiastic voice were weaving a message of hope, of direction, and most importantly, of confidence in us. Over and over again, Father would encourage us to "make a decision" about something we needed to do in our life. "Act," he would say. "Make a decision." And then, after encouraging us to make a decision, he would make the following statement with the firmness and resolve that washed through us like a driving rain and inspired us like a brilliant sunrise: "You Can Do It."

He must have said "Make a decision" and "You can do it" thirty times in that twenty minute message. His words resonated through the church. His message stuck. We left church that day believing two things: we needed to make some decisions and that we could do it. We believed that we could achieve anything that we put our minds to. Father's inspirational message stays with us to this day. His words still echo in thoughts and decisions, and his belief is captured in the pages of this book.

So here's the catch. Yes, there is a catch.

Before moving on and reading the remaining chapters of this book, you will need to make a decision. And then, at the end of the book, you will need to make another decision. Two decisions are all we require. They are not complicated, but they are important.

Here is the first decision that you will need to make: You need to decide to keep an open mind as you read the rest of this book. That's it. That's the decision. Keep an open mind to learn new things. Keep an open mind to question and test what you have learned in the past and believe today. Keep an open mind to question and test what is written in this book. Socrates wrote that "wisdom begins in wonder." Lifetimes later, Einstein said, "The important thing is not to stop questioning." Both Socrates and Einstein understood the importance of continuous learning and exploration. Heed their advice and open your mind to learning. It is a simple decision to make. It is an important decision to make. You can do it.

The remaining chapters of this book describe eight important attributes that are shared by people who live extraordinary, wonderful lives and people who achieve their dreams. Alone, each attribute is powerful and potent. When a person works to develop all of these attributes, to learn and grow, they can accomplish extraordinary things; they can achieve dreams; they can become leaders.

The attributes described in the following chapters are not listed or ranked by importance. They are attributes that fit together and work together and are of equal importance to each other. They are the pieces of a roadmap that will take you places you want to go. They are guideposts to living an extraordinary life.

You have made your decision. So let's begin.

You can do it.

Chapter 3

The Attribute of Enthusiasm

"Enthusiasm moves the world."
-Arthur James Balfour

Definition
Enthusiasm, n. 1. Great excitement for or interest in a subject or cause. 2. A source or cause of great excitement or interest.

Synonyms
Passion; Fervor; Gusto; Zeal; Zest; Eagerness; Interest; Keenness;

Related Words/Phrases
Positive; Positive Mental Attitude; Optimistic; Upbeat; Energy,

Edna was a ray of sunshine that permeated a bleak, small, windowless, cramped cubicle farm. Her cubicle was positioned near the entrance to the small space that housed the offices of twelve people. There was no way into or out of the office without passing by her open cubicle. She was an experienced salesperson, but more significantly, she was the unofficial matriarch of the entire sales organization.

No one knew her age. No one dared to ask. Edna had been selling for a long time, and had achieved recognition as the top salesperson in the city. Along with that respect came a don't ask, don't tell status as it related to age. It may have been the subject over lunch, or an office pool for entertainment purposes only, but it was never discussed openly in front of the leader of the pack.

A co-worker's first exposure to Edna usually occurred on the Monday of their first day of employment. Edna was always the first person in the office. As a new employee would walk into the office, he would of course make their way past Edna's cubicle. And then, he would be greeted. "Good morning! Happy Monday!" would ring out from this small woman in a singing, optimistic way that could not be duplicated even by the best mimic.

Edna didn't just greet new people this way. She greeted everyone this way, and not just on Monday-- every day, day in and day out. These were not empty words. Edna lived these words.

Edna had been asked countless times to move into sales management. Each time, she would politely decline, saying that selling was her passion. Each year, she would make more money. And each year, as companies are sometimes known to do, management would find a way to reduce her income by giving accounts to other salespeople. Each year, Edna would sell more, and find a way to make as much if not more money that she did the year before. She would do it with a smile on her face, and rampant enthusiasm in her heart.

Edna's enthusiasm was contagious. With her passion and optimism, Edna could melt the heart of even the most grizzled customer. When the company floundered, she rallied. While other salespeople struggled with selling a declining product, Edna's enthusiasm persevered, and so did her income.

Edna's enthusiasm for her work and for life carried her to level of success that many aspire to. One day, a junior salesperson who was struggling with some difficult news asked her a question that many had wondered: "How do you stay so positive in the face of all this tough news?" She stopped what she was doing and looked into the eyes of the young salesperson. She answered, "It really is very simple. I keep my head down, I work hard, and I smile." Edna's enthusiasm was at the very core of her success. Edna lives a wonderful life.

"Enthusiasm is a vital element toward the individual success of every man or woman."
-Conrad Hilton

Typically, people are drawn to enthusiastic people. Do you remember the first time you met a truly enthusiastic person, a person whose positive nature was clearly evident? It could have been a teacher who was passionate about a subject, or a coach who was eager to teach you and help you improve. In many cases it may have been a childhood friend who was sharing her eagerness with a new toy, game or sport. Do you remember how that person's enthusiasm made you feel? It may be that teacher or coach sparked an interest in something that you hold important to this day. It may be that your childhood friend sparked in an interest in a game or sport that you then became interested in, or had to have.

Kids, Adults And Enthusiasm

Kids are excellent models of enthusiastic behavior. Their enthusiasm can, especially when they are young, know no bounds. Picture the swarming mass of young kids just starting to play the game of soccer and trailing a ball around the field. No form, no function, just squeals of delight as the ball travels across the field followed by the pack. The coach's enthusiasm may wane as she tries to teach basic skills, but not the pack. For them, it's the thrill of the chase and the joy of the kick. Childlike enthusiasm is inspiring, and even scary. "Where do they get that energy and enthusiasm?" we ask.

As we get older, it becomes harder to maintain that level of enthusiasm. Our lives become more complex and our responsibilities become more cumbersome. We have to make very difficult decisions every day. We have to work, to study, to go out with our friends, to take care of our children. We are taking care of our parents, volunteering at school, traveling for days on end for business, trying to lose weight, attempting to exercise, cleaning the house, cutting the lawn, and trying to figure out how to pay all of the bills. Who has the energy to be enthusiastic?!

Did someone decide that we have to become less enthusiastic as we get older? No. It just happens to some people. As we grow older, we lose touch with some of our childlike qualities that would serve us well throughout life. It would be wonderful if we could carry attributes and qualities like enthusiasm, a sense of wonder, the ability to belly laugh until it hurts, questioning what we don't understand, and faith into adulthood.

It is an admirable goal to instill in our children the importance of remaining childlike, not childish, for the remainder of their life, to exhibit enthusiasm and passion for the things that they care about. Those people who are successful in today's world and live wonderful lives have found ways to maintain and even grow their childlike enthusiasm.

"If you are not getting as much from life as you want to, then examine your state of enthusiasm."
-Norman Vincent Peale

It was a 6:15am flight from Indianapolis to Denver. Due to extra security, that meant a 4:30am arrival at the airport. Ouch, that's early. It was two weeks before school was scheduled to begin and that meant that tons of families were trying to get that one last trip in before the hectic school year began. Early morning and crowds of families-- not a good combination.

Luggage checked and kids in tow, hundreds of people now waited for the security check. Instructions said to form two lines, and in the early morning hours, the family shepards led their sheep willingly into the lines. It was too early for a struggle or an argument. The group did as it was told. The lines were quiet except for the occasional cell phone ring or the cry of a cranky young passenger. Lines full of sullen faces; it was too early to be excited, enthusiastic, or even pleasant.

In the distance, the lone figure of an airport policeman strolled between the two lines. As he made his way between the two lines of dreariness, he would smile and talk to families.

"My lines are always the best lines," he would say with pride. "My lines always have the nicest people."

"Straighten up team," was the command from the smiling officer, "and smile for the cameras."

A small boy standing in line with his parents and three other siblings was about to let the world know that he was not happy to be there when the officer, sensing meltdown, approached.

"And who is this handsome gentleman?" the officer said with a big smile. "Are you headed someplace fun?" The rumble averted, the officer continued down the line with countless "good mornings" and encouragement for the ragged group.

As the line moved slowly forward, an odd buzz seemed to emanate from the group. People were actually speaking to one another. People were smiling. People were engaging one another and the officer in good-natured teasing. And for a moment, people actually seemed pleased to be traveling and heading to their destination and all because one man showed enthusiasm for his work and had the courage to share his enthusiasm.

How many lives did that one man positively impact that morning? Interestingly enough, when that story was shared with someone who travels often through the Indianapolis airport, the comments was made: "Oh yeah, I know that guy. He's great. He actually makes it ok to fly." That's one enthusiastic person, making a very real difference.

The Power of Enthusiasm

In 1967 Dr. Norman Vincent Peale felt that the attribute of enthusiasm was so important, it deserved a book devoted totally to the discussion of developing and maintaining this powerful force. His belief was that enthusiasm could make a difference in how one's life turned out.

Enthusiasm is the force behind turning obstacles into opportunities. It is the power that we draw on when challenges and difficulties weigh upon us and we search for solutions. Enthusiasm has the power to attract and persuade. Best of all, enthusiasm is something that we alone control, and no person or organization can take our enthusiasm away from us because it is a product of our mental attitude.

Our mental attitude is one of, if not *the* significant factor that determines the ultimate outcome of our life. Mental attitude influences the friends we make, the successes we enjoy and the legacy we leave behind. The development of a mental attitude built on the foundation of enthusiasm is critically important to those who wish to live wonderful lives and achieve the extraordinary.

"Enthusiasm glows, radiates, permeates and immediately captures everyone's interest."
-Paul J. Meyer

Is enthusiasm still relevant today? Absolutely. In fact, enthusiasm is more important than ever.

Life is more complicated and challenges seem to have greater risk attached. Lack of job creation in our economy makes it difficult for those whose positions have been eliminated. Off-shoring may shrink white collar jobs the way downsizing affected jobs in decades previous. School districts cut programs because of funding issues. That's why today's leading experts on organizational and personal growth speak to enthusism and optimism in their writing.

Enthusiasm and Success

Successful people, people who achieve dreams and lead extraordinary lives, understand the value of enthusiasm. Enthusiastic people set the pace. It is difficult for anyone to gripe or slow down a process if the people they work with on a daily basis set an enthusiastic, positive pace. Enthusiasm is infectious. People like to be around enthusiastic people. Enthusiastic people attract other enthusiastic, successful people. Enthusiastic people use challenges as stepping stones to opportunity. Enthusiastic people set themselves apart in a positive way.

Take a look around at successful people that you know and respect and spend some time studying successful people in history. What do they share in common? How do the successful and happy people that you know display their enthusiasm? How do they use their enthusiasm to overcome obstacles? By paying attention to those around you who exhibit enthusiasm on a consistent basis, you can learn to capture those same skills and develop your own, unique ways to make enthusiasm work for you.

Being an enthusiastic person does not come without challenges. It takes courage to be enthusiastic. You may be challenged by those around you who would prefer not to have their mediocre world rocked. Some may call you false or challenge your sincerity. Others may accuse you of "sucking up to the boss" or accuse you of trying to get ahead. Remain committed, and with practice, you will absolutely persevere. Many, many successful people, who have achieved great honor and riches, have been chastised for their enthusiasm and for their dreams. By remaining enthusiastic, you can succeed, fulfill your dreams, live a wonderful life, and most importantly, make the lives of those around you extraordinary.

Enthusiasm Prevails

The young account executive was talking with her boss about the recent addition to the sales team. She was concerned because the new employee did not seem to be fitting into the team, and she had stepped forward to share her thoughts.

"What do you think the problem is?" the sales manager asked the account executive.

"Well," said the account executive thoughtfully, "He just doesn't seem to be fitting in. I really think it has to do with his annoying enthusiasm for his job and life. I mean, really, no one is really like that. It just rubs people the wrong way."

The sales manager replied, "It rubs everyone the wrong way?"

"Well, I guess I can't speak for *everyone,*" noted the account executive, "but it certainly annoys me."

The young, enthusiastic salesperson could have backed down. In order to fit in, he could have let go of his youthful enthusiasm and slipped into the popular world of mediocrity. The good news is that he didn't. He stayed his course. He helped others find reasons to be enthusiastic. He shared his passion for selling and for life with others. Over time, he became the most respected and successful member of the sales team. Today, he's living a dream, having found success and happiness at a young age, with a brilliant future ahead of him. As for the annoyed peer, it turned out a little differently. She soon found herself out of the selling profession, failing to achieve a level of acceptable success.

Developing the attribute of enthusiasm will help you lead a wonderful life and achieve your dreams and goals. It is a decision that you can make for yourself. This is something that only you control. The power of enthusiasm is locked away inside of you. It does not need to be purchased. It is not a genetic gift. Enthusiasm does not belong only to members of a certain club or come with a specific degree from an anointed university. The attribute of enthusiasm is yours to use, waiting to be harnessed, practiced and enjoyed.

Seeking The Enthusiastic You

There are many, many ways to develop and improve your level of enthusiasm. The key is to start. The development of enthusiasm, and in fact all of the key attributes discussed in this book, take time, practice and patience. People who are living wonderful lives, finding success, happiness and riches beyond their imagination did not wake up one day and find themselves dripping with enthusiasm. Unfortunately, the Enthusiasm Fairy is a myth. Successful people work at being enthusiastic every day.

We will give you three ways to start developing and improving your level of enthusiasm. These are simple, proven ways to get started. In fact, they are so simple that you may dismiss them as silly and a waste of time. Don't. Simple ideas put into practice over time can become habit. Positive habits lead to personal growth. Personal growth will lead to sustained success and happiness.

Idea #1: Find an Enthusiasm Mentor

Seek out the most consistently enthusiastic person that you know. This should be someone that you admire for their enthusiasm as well as for the quality of their life. Tell them that you would like to work on your level of enthusiasm, and ask them if they would be willing to serve as a model for you. Ask them questions about their attitudes and how they grew their enthusiasm. Question them on how they maintain their enthusiasm when faced with difficult situations and tough challenges. Ask them about their failures in trying to maintain their enthusiasm. Study their behavior and their speech. Imitate some of the things that they do, and behaviors that you feel comfortable with that mesh with your personality. Work to make those behaviors your own. Keep a log, journal or blog of what you learn.

Idea #2: Try Smiling

Smiles, like enthusiasm, are infectious. This is a simple, painless way to start down the road of developing the attribute of enthusiasm in your life. Begin each day with a smile; first thing out of bed, smile at yourself in the mirror. Study your smile. Is it a broad, see-my-teeth smile? Or is it a thin I'm-up-to-something smile? How does this make you feel? Silly or stupid? Well, then put some clothes on and try again. Make it a practice to begin greeting each person that you meet and speak to with a smile. If you forget, don't worry about it. Start over. Remember, no matter what's on your mind or what problems you are having at the moment, begin each conversation with a smile. Make note of how this makes you feel, and as important, how people around you begin to respond. Capture that feeling and build on it.

Idea #3: Pick Something, Write it Down, Set a Goal

Is there something in your life that you really enjoy doing that you have not done in some time? For example, let's say you love to take a thirty-minute run outdoors. When you run, your head clears and the problems of the day fade away. Running makes you feel good.

Go for a run and savor every moment. Take time to notice how you feel. Notice the trees, the flowers and the dog chasing you down the street. Make a mental note of that great feeling. Take a pen and paper and write down a few words that describe the feeling. Then, set your goal. "I will take at least fifteen minutes a day to capture this feeling." Keep the small piece of paper with your words and your goal on it with you at all times. Read it when you wake up in the morning (after you smile) and before you go to bed at night.

Try at least one of these ideas for the next thirty days.

You can do it!

Chapter 4

The Attribute of Positive Communication

"A good listener is not only popular everywhere, but after a while he knows something."
-Wilson Mizner

<u>Definition</u>
Communication, n. 1. The act of communicating 2. The exchange of thoughts, messages, or information

<u>Synonyms</u>
Message, announcement, statement, letter, e-mail, phone call

<u>Related Words/Phrases</u>
Listen, speak, debate, argue, convince, engage in conversation, presentation

    Successful people, people who live wonderful lives and achieve their dreams, communicate effectively and clearly. They understand that effective communication centers on the important balance of listening and conveying ideas. For example, Stephen Covey understands the significant role of communication in the development of personal character, and the importance of balance in communication, which he highlights in his fantastic book *The Seven Habits of Highly Effective People*. Stephen

Covey gets it. There are others who understand as well. Unfortunately, when it comes to communication, there still is a great deal of focus put on the spoken and written word, and frankly, not enough on the power of listening.

The Great Communicator

Here's a quick history quiz. Who was known as "The Great Communicator?" If you answered Ronald Reagan, you are correct. President Reagan was given this label because of his genuine gift of delivering the spoken word in a style and manner that communicated clearly and persuaded very effectively. He was an eloquent and powerful speaker. People believed what he was saying and believed in him.

Unfortunately, there is not much, if anything, written about Reagan's listening skills. Nor is there much written about the listening skills of other great leaders. Scan the bookshelves at your favorite bookseller or browse the Internet. You will see many, many book titles featuring great speeches and communication throughout history. (We can't wait for the release of "Great Memo's and emails of our time!" Now there's a thriller.)

We don't always know what the great leaders of America heard to inspire such grand rhetoric. Missing from the bookshelves are works titled "What I heard Gorbachev say" or "As I was listening to Kruschev." While this is certainly meant tongue in cheek, it is written to stress the point that listening, the often overlooked skill, is as important to overall communication as speaking effectively. And without question, to be an effective communicator, one must practice both.

Our goal then is to become "Ultimate Communicators"-- effective listeners and communicators of thoughts and ideas. You may be better at one or the other. It may be that you have never given thought to practicing either. No problem. If your ultimate goal is to live a wonderful life and achieve your dreams (or get a better job, improve a relationship or lose a few pounds), you can begin today working on both sides of this important attribute.

The remainder of this chapter is divided into two parts: in Part 1, we will cover effective listening. In Part 2, we will discuss outward, positive communication.

Part I- Listening

A husband and wife are sitting in the family room, relaxing after having both endured a long day at work. The television is on in the background and the kids are running around somewhere downstairs exerting their last bit of energy before heading to bed. There is a conversation of sorts taking place, with the wife telling her husband about the discussion she had that day with their son's teacher.

"And so she feels that if Timmy applied himself more and focused in class, his grades would improve," says the woman in a tired voice.

Silence.

"Honey, what do you think about what I just said?" she asks.

"Hmmm?" comes the quiet reply.

"You didn't hear a word I just said, did you?" questions the now perturbed spouse.

"I heard everything you just said dear" is the answer from the all-knowing, all-seeing, can read *and* watch TV with his eyes closed husband. Sure, he may have heard something. But because he was not actively listening, he didn't *understand* a word.

Sound familiar? Have you been in a conversation like this recently? Unfortunately, communication like this is taking place in homes, businesses and meeting rooms around the world. It's not unusual, and it has been happening since a human uttered his first word. Some historians believe that the first word uttered by a human was "fire." We are certain that the second word uttered was "huh?"

The skills involved in communicating, effective listening and the communication of our ideas, are the most significant life skills we learn. Unfortunately, while we spend years learning to read and write effectively, very little time is devoted to the development of our ability to listen effectively. The skills that we do learn are often listening tricks, surface methods used to convey the act of listening which end up usually insulting the person being listened to because of their transparency. Our ultimate success depends on our capacity to balance these communication skills. Successful people are effective listeners.

All wise men share one trait in common: the ability to listen.
-Frank Tyger

There are issues with listening in all facets of life and they impact our ability to succeed in relationships and business.

Open mouth...insert foot.

Take the example of a young manager who was promoted to a new facility from another location for which he worked. He was nervous and highly self conscious of his age and minimal experience. The people who worked for him knew nothing of him or his reputation prior to his arrival. When he made his first appearance, he called everybody together and lectured for forty-five minutes in his effort to prove his knowledge and competence. His audience reacted, however, in a very noncommittal, reserved way. They walked away from the first meeting, having listened to him for a considerable amount of time. The workers had not been given the opportunity to raise questions, voice concerns or make their observations about the way the new location was running. The new general manager's intent to prove his competence by talking about all of his experience worked against him. In fact, he alienated the people he was trying so hard to please.

To grow personally and to achieve dreams, we all need to become more effective listeners and communicators.

To become an effective listener, it is important to understand the definition of real, active, empathetic listening. Listening is active attending to what another is saying. It means listening with the intent to understand. We're not talking about surface understanding here. We are talking about understanding from another person's perspective, from her point of view. It is an understanding of not only how she feels, but *why* she feels the way that she does. Does this sound like something that will take practice? It should. With practice, you can become an effective listener.

Effective listeners express interest in people, demonstrate their attention to the individual and communicate a realistic patience (which, by the way, is not always easy when listening to a teenager). Effective listeners minimize the chance of interruption from telephones, emails, friends and/or family members.

Active, empathetic listening requires that you attend to both what a person is saying and *how* she is saying it. Be responsive, and listen not only with your ears, but with your mind and your heart. Ask questions, making sure that the questions are short, open-ended questions which call for explanation and elaboration rather than questions which are leading and seeking conclusion.

It takes patience to listen effectively. Waiting to speak while someone finishes an idea, rather than completing a person's statement, requires time. You should not try to anticipate the question, phrase or judgment, but rather pay attention and listen with ears, mind and heart to what the person is saying and feeling.

"No man would listen to you talk if he didn't know it was his turn next."
-Edgar Watson Howe

Effective, empathetic listening can be difficult. Yet, to work toward our goal of becoming the "Ultimate Communicator" we will need to travel some difficult paths. For example, let's take communicating with a teenager.

Talk To The Hand Dad

First, there's the language barrier. Then, in many cases, there's the age barrier. Add in the relevance barrier and you have enough obstacles to set up a course. But with patient listening and a will to succeed, we can learn a great deal from our conversations with our teenage children.

For example, the statements "My life sucks" or "I hate school," may actually mean "I'm afraid or scared of a situation that I don't know how to handle." How you respond to the first two statements may well decide if you get to the real meaning of the teen's statement. Listen without making a judgment. And as significantly, listen without projecting your own life or life history into the conversation at first.

To those of us working to live a wonderful life and achieve dreams, listening is an incredibly important skill and powerful tool. It is the salesperson's ultimate instrument. It is the teacher's resource. It is a manager's asset used to determine what motivates and drives employees and how to improve business. It is the parents' resource for understanding their children and for letting their children know that they are important. It is a friend's gift.

Part II- Positive, Outward Communication

A thirteen-year-old boy had been playing football for five years. Although he had many interests, football was his passion. He played wide receiver on offense and defensive end on defense-- an odd combination, but it worked. He played every play of the game, and he participated with reckless abandon. He was small and his skills were average at best. It didn't matter. He loved the game, he loved being on the field with his friends, and he loved the thrill of competing and winning. The game that he looked forward to most each year was against the cross town rival, and it was always the last game of the year.

This particular year, the cross town rival had added a running back who was faster than any player they had ever seen, and the opposing team was using his speed to their advantage at every opportunity.

Our young football player was seeing a lot of action and loving every minute. He had caught one pass and made a few tackles. Then, things started to go wrong. The opposing team was on offense, and had started a play that ran away from the young defensive end. Following his instincts, he ran after the ball carrier in hot pursuit. And then, it happened. Before he could react, the one halfback handed the ball to another halfback moving in the opposite direction. With a blaze of speed, the opposing team's secret weapon ran right past our defensive end for a twenty-yard gain. They had tricked him with a reverse. He couldn't believe his eyes.

As he ran back to the huddle shaking his head, he heard his coach yell to him from the sideline, "Stay at home." Two plays later, the same thing happened. The same pursuit, the same blaze of speed, the same sinking feeling and another twenty-yard gain. Once again, he heard the words from his coach as he ran back to the huddle, "I said stay at home!"

And then, the unthinkable happened. They called the exact same play again. After a third episode of watching blazing speed run past his defensive end, the coach had no choice.

The coach called his player off the field and sent in a substitute. The young defensive end was crushed. He had never missed a play before. He had never been called off the field. From his young perspective, life, as he knew it, was over.

The Coach called his player over to him with a great deal of urgency and passion in his voice. He pulled the boy's face up close to his, holding the boy's facemask to insure attention.

"What don't you understand about staying at home?" the coach questioned with great passion.

The boy was reeling. He was scared. He was honest in his answer.

"I don't understand anything about it, Coach!" the boy sputtered.

"Excuse me?" the coach said with more than slight bewilderment.

"I don't understand because no one ever taught me what stay at home means," confessed the boy.

Reality set in. The coach let go of the young player's facemask and put his hands on his shoulder pads. He spoke in a softer, yet still urgent tone.

"It's simple," he began. "You are a defensive end. Your job is to contain. That means your job is to let no one, ever get around you. Here's what I want you to do. The next time the ball is snapped, I want you to take three steps over the line of scrimmage, turn slightly in, and stand there. If the ball is coming your way, then make the tackle. However, if the ball is going the other way, I want you to stay where you are and count to five. Then, you can chase the ball. Do you understand?"

"Yes Coach!"

"Then get back in there."

Only two plays had run during those instructions. The two plays were costly, as the arch rivals had marched down to the home team's 10 yard line. There was time for one play before the half as our newly-instructed defensive end ran back on the field.

"Stay at home, stay at home, stay at home," he repeated to himself.

The ball was snapped, and the defensive end took three steps across the line of scrimmage and turned his body in. The ball was going the other way. Every instinct in his body wanted to chase that running back.

"Stay at home, stay at home, stay at home," a voice in his head kept saying.

One thousand one. The ball was moving away from him quickly. One thousand two. Wait, there was something going on in the backfield of the opposing team. One thousand three. The halfback with the ball just handed it to the halfback with lightening speed, who was now running the other way, right at our defensive end. One thousand four.

Bam. The halfback was stunned. The entire opposing team was stunned. The play that had worked for an entire half of the game had just resulted in a ten-yard loss as our defensive end made the tackle and stopped a touchdown. The whistle blew to end the first half.

The only person who was not stunned by what happened, the Coach, ran out onto the field, lifted his young defensive end up in celebration, and carried him off the field in joy.

"Mastery of language affords remarkable power."
-Frantz Fanon

Positive, effective communication is powerful. It can teach, explain and motivate. It can contribute to mending a broken relationship and it can inspire nations to greatness. The key to the power of outward communication lies in its effective creation and delivery.

The majority of outward communication can be divided into three basic types: the spoken word such as speeches, conversation, lyrics associated with music and verbal instruction; the written word such as books, magazines, newspapers, email, text and instant messaging; and, visual communication such as body language and visual images in pictures and movies.

Try as we might, we cannot control a persons ultimate understanding of our communication. We do not have power to control someone's ability to listen, or his mood, background, and life experiences. It is very important for a positive, effective communicator to take these issues into account when planning and delivering a message. With hard work and practice, you can overcome many of the obstacles that are outside of your control. The key to success is developing useful communication skills that will allow you to build positive, effective messages.

The term positive communication can conjure up many images. When hearing the word "positive" in relation to communication, one may think of Pollyanna and her sweet messages that don't contain a negative thought or sound. Can you hear someone talking to a new puppy when seeing it for the first time? While most everyone has expressed emotion in this way at some point in their life, that's not what we are talking about.

Positive communication can be passionate. Positive communication can stem from joy, happiness, disappointment and even anger. The key to making communication positive and effective is building a message that conveys proactive thought, instruction, or ideas that are delivered in a tone that will be well received and understood.

My Boss Thinks I'm An Idiot

A manager asks her employee to write a memo explaining the company's new vacation policy to the staff. Once completed, the employee brings the memo to the manager for her review. As the manager reads the memo, she becomes increasingly disappointed with her employee's efforts. The manager does not like the format of the memo and feels that the information is incomplete. She turns to her employee and yells, "This is terrible. Are you an idiot? No one will understand this." Our upset manager follows with instructions for making the memo more effective. However, those instructions are most likely lost on the employee, who is reeling from the manager's initial statement.

Instead of listening effectively and learning, the employee is probably thinking about calling the manager a few words that make the word idiot look tame.

Does this sound like an extreme example? It's not. Communication like this happens all the time in businesses, schools and homes. It's a cycle of communication that can bring about unhappiness on the job, distance in relationships and a lack of interest in learning.

Our manager could have turned this from a negative experience into a positive opportunity for learning by simply changing the way she began the conversation. For example, saying "I appreciate the work that you have put into this so far. I think that there are some changes that *we* can make to further clarify the policy. Let me give you some ideas…" sets the tone for constructive dialogue, criticism and instruction.

Positive, effective outward communication begins by understanding as much as you can about the person or group that will receive the message. The understanding of another person's point of view or a group's issues and background will help you communicate your views effectively.

If our ultimate goal is for our ideas to be appreciated, respected, adopted or obeyed, the communication of those ideas must be understood. By conveying in your communication that you understand someone's point of view or ideas, you can often keep that person from building the walls that prohibit open dialogue and understanding.

"If you are patient in one moment of anger, you will escape a hundred days of sorrow"
-Chinese Proverb

Have you ever been yelled at or screamed at by another person? Besides getting your attention, how did it make you feel? The tone of communication has a great deal to do with its effectiveness. While yelling and screaming at someone surely can get their attention, except in certain very specific circumstances, raised voices are not effective in the long term for effective communication. Typically, communicating in a normal tone of voice with fluctuations for emotions like joy, anger and disappointment is the most effective way to insure that your message will be heard and understood.

Are there exceptions? Sure. If you are standing in the front yard and watching your two- year-old begin to run into the street, yelling to attract his attention would be more than appropriate. If you are at a football game and your friends are yelling and cheering after a touchdown, it would seem odd if you said "Go team" in a conversational voice. Taking a positive tone and speaking in a normal voice for a majority of your outward communication will not only help your messages to be effectively communicated, but it will also make those times when you must raise your voice seem that much more important.

People who understand the significance of tone in their communication and who consistently communicate in a positive, natural voice have ideas that are heard and understood. These same people live wonderful lives and achieve dreams.

"Remember not only to say the right thing in the right place, but far more difficult still, to leave unsaid the wrong thing at the tempting moment."
-Benjamin Franklin

There are several tools for positive, effective communication that you can work to develop.

The Tool of Relevance

Have you ever been talking with someone who rambles on and on about things that you are just not interested in? You find yourself thinking about your next meeting, reviewing your grocery list, continuing to read a magazine while on the phone, or instant messaging/emailing a friend? Are you a bad listener? Or, is the person doing the talking simply not an effective communicator because she doesn't understand the tool of relevance?

The tool of relevance deals with communicating messages in which the receiving party has interest, or making sure that the communication is relevant to their lives. The next time you are having a conversation with someone, test yourself. How are your ideas and your conversation relevant to the other person's life? (Answering "It's important to me so it should be important to them" doesn't cut it.)

The Tool of Motivation

What makes another person tick? What motivates and inspires the person? What calls another person to action? Motivation and relevance are tied together in effective communication. If you can find out what is important in the person's life (relevance) and what rewards or drives a person (motivation), you can effectively build communication that can make a difference.

The Tools of Purpose and Clarity

With relevance and motivation, we have what's important to a person and what will cause him to act. The next tools involve building a clear message that has purpose. These are simple, but very important tools.

All of our communication should have a purpose. Our purpose could be to make someone laugh, to teach, to inspire or to show love. Our message should be built around our purpose, and it should be clear and specific with words and sentences that are easily understandable. How many times have you bought something that needs to be assembled, opened the assembly instructions, and pulled your hair out because the instructions were impossible to follow? Communication without purpose or clarity will cause the same response in people with whom you are communicating.

The Tool of Silence

Silence is rare in business and homes. However, it can be an incredibly powerful tool. Periods of silence can be emotional. Recall the quiet, stern look of a disapproving teacher. A painful silence. Time stretched endlessly as the pressure built. Silence can help to make a point of conversation powerful. The use of silence in communication can also help us to listen and better understand a person's point of view. Wait for meaningful responses after presenting an idea or feeling. People will often elaborate or share their ideas, if for no other reason than to release the tension they feel from silence.

Successful people who live wonderful lives and achieve their dreams understand the power of listening and positive outward communication. Some were given gifts of beautiful voices or stage presence. Others were not. Some people had parents, teachers or mentors who taught them effective listening skills. Some did not. You do not have to be born with these skills to be successful.

The key is to develop the attribute of positive, effective communication. Start today. You can do it. We will give you three ways to develop and improve your ability to listen and communicate effectively. These are simple, proven ways to get started and/or improve.

Idea # 1: A Listening Checklist

Rate yourself on the following effective listening behaviors. You can also ask someone close to you or someone you work with to rate you on each of the following behaviors and see how well you perceive yourself. These are also the behaviors which should be practiced regularly.

	Poor	Below Average	Average	Above Average	Excellent
As a listener, are your questions Clear and concise?					
Do your listener's interruptions disrupt the speaker's trend of thought?					
As a listener, can you rephrase accurately what a person has said?					
Do you give people a chance to talk without external interruptions?					

Do you dominate conversations?					
As a listener, are you judgmental?					
Do you seem interested in the speaker? (show head nod, rephrase)					
Are you attentive to what is being said?					
Do you, as the listener, talk to much?					
As a listener, are you easily approached by others?					

Idea #2: Shut Up and Listen

Effective listening takes a great deal of practice. It also takes patience, because typically it's much more fun to tell your friends about your weekend adventures than it is to listen to their stories.

This idea will require you to practice your listening skills (and will undoubtedly test your patience). Once a day, for the next thirty days, focus on listening effectively and practicing your listening skills in one conversation. Because we are only asking you to pay special attention to one conversation (that said, you should listen all the time) make sure that is an important conversation with someone you trust and who will be honest with you.

After the person is done sharing his idea, repeat back to the person in summary form what they just communicated. Then, ask them if you communicated their idea correctly. Listen to the answer. If you missed the point, try to determine where your listening process derailed.

Practice this type of effective listening once a day for thirty days, and then adopt the skills you learn into all of your communication.

Idea #3: Practice Clarity

Communication that is clear has a much better chance of being understood than communication that is not focused and confusing. Makes sense and sounds easy, doesn't it? And yet, it is astounding how much of the communication in our lives today lacks clarity. You can practice clarity in your communication.

First, find someone who is willing to work with you and help you develop this skill. It could be a co-worker, your teenager or a close friend. They have to be willing to be honest with you and you have to be willing to accept honest, constructive criticism.

Next, develop an idea, thought or instruction that you would like to convey. Write it down as clearly as you can. The next step is to have your partner in communication read the text.

Finally, they should, without the benefit of paper, explain back to you what you were trying to communicate. Ask them how you could have made your communication more clear and understandable. (No cheating. Writing down "Take out the garbage" or "Clean your room" and handing it to your teenage son is not in the spirit of this exercise. Writing out full instructions for cleaning is admissible and encouraged!)

Try at least one of these ideas for the next thirty days. You can do it!

Chapter 5

The Attribute of Focus

"Concentration is the secret of strengths in politics, in war, in trade, in short in all management of human affairs."
-Ralph Waldo Emerson

Definition
Focus, (as a noun) 2a. The distinctness or clarity of an image rendered by an optical system. 2b. Adjustment for distinctness or clarity. 3. A center of interest or activity. (as a verb) 3. To concentrate (on)

Synonyms
(As a noun) focal point, center, spotlight, concentration, motivation
(As a verb) concentrate, direct, converge, bring together

Related Words/Phrases
Mission, Purpose, Area of Concentration

Most people in America have either been on a low carb diet or know someone who has tried a version of this popular diet trend. Interestingly enough, low carbohydrate diets have been around for years. Only recently has the phrase "low carb" and the diets associated with the phrase become standard household words. Can you think of other words or phrases like this? In business, it was terms like re-engineering and total quality, and there are many other examples. There are words, phrases, trends and concepts in life and business that become heavily used as the trend of the moment. The hot word or phrase is then overused, and finally it vanishes or fades away as a new trend takes over.

Focus Factor Fades

Something similar to this pattern happened with the word and concept of focus. Several books with the word focus in the title were written in the mid to late 90's through 2002 by some of the best marketing and motivation minds in business. Over that period of time, the concept and word were hot. Now, in the year 2004, one executive was overheard saying that the word "focus" was overused and not current.

The new, hip concepts/phrases in business are "viral marketing," "buzz marketing," "sneezers," and "behavioral marketing." Today, people might ask you if you are leading a life of purpose, or if your cheese has been moved. Hanging in the hallways of schools you may see posters about making work fun tied to a current business bestseller. We do not dismiss any of these concepts as unimportant or not meaningful. Quite the contrary, they all have value in personal and professional growth.

The word focus may not be used as often today in conjunction with personal and professional growth, but do not be quick to dismiss the power of this attribute. The influence and importance of focus in life has been documented through the ages; from Biblical scripture and the theories of Sun Tzu, to the modern era teachings of Napoleon Hill, Stephen Covey and others, focus has been a core principle in teaching about human achievement.

"Most people have no idea of the giant capacity we can immediately command when we focus all of our resources on mastering a single area of our lives."
-Tony Robbins

Thomas Edison, Henry Ford, Helen Keller, Abraham Lincoln, Oprah Winfrey and Larry Bird all share the common attribute of focus. There are many people who can be added to this list. They are people who cross all boundaries of decades, age, gender, race and religion. In their efforts to achieve they have failed numerous times. Ultimately, whether they are a famous statesman, a wealthy entrepreneur, a television celebrity, or your next door neighbor, their ability to focus and remain focused has played an instrumental role in their living a wonderful life and achieving their dreams.

Here is some great news! You too have the ability to develop the attribute of focus and use it in combination with the other seven attributes to live an extraordinary life. While there are always several factors involved in the successful development of attributes, as it pertains to focus, there are two key factors: decision making and practicing concentration.

Distractions

Before we begin making decisions, it is important to take a look around at people we know. We have all known someone who is involved in so many projects, tasks or hobbies that they never seem to do any of them well. There are also people we know who can't seem to make up their minds and drift from one interest, job or relationship to another without finding fulfillment, happiness or success. And then, there are the friends, relatives or co-workers that we have who ramble incessantly in conversations, switching from topic to topic like a bee pollinating flowers in a garden; we couldn't begin to summarize the conversation because we don't know where to start. Do you see parts of yourself in any of these people?

In recent times, behavior like this is very often blamed on ADHD. We are not intending to debate the existence or validity of ADHD, or discuss treatment. We do suggest that for many people who are not living happy, fulfilled, wonderful lives and not achieving their dreams, their simple inability to focus is holding them back.

The first step for growth in this area is simple. Make the decision to become more focused. Make a commitment to yourself and to a partner, if it is appropriate. Once you have made this commitment and you really intend to keep it, you can move forward.

"Concentrate on finding your goal, then concentrate on reaching it."
-Colonel Michael Friedman

While the first step of making a decision to become more focused is relatively simple, the next two steps require more thought, courage and practice.

Your Point of Focus

Outside forces begin to shape our focus from the time we are very young. Every young child has been asked at one time or another "What do you want to be when you grow up?" The answer usually depends on the last toy played with or the parents' occupations and it can change by the minute. As we get into high school, we are asked by parents, teachers and counselors about our interests so that we can attend a college that is strong in that area. In college, we are asked "What are you majoring in?" by friends and family. Every so often the answer "undecided" would emerge and the listener would flinch as if just given bad news. Finally, as we enter the working world, we are asked the same question in interview after interview: "Where do you see yourself in five years?"

There is nothing wrong with changing your mind as a child every five minutes, and going to a good liberal arts college and getting a general liberal arts degree, as long as it is understood that to live an extraordinary life and achieve our dreams, at some point we will need to make a decision that gives clarity and focus to our lives.

What are your talents? What are you passionate about? What are your dreams? These are questions that you need to answer, or at least begin to answer. Can your dreams and aspirations change? Absolutely. If you are focused and passionately following a dream or goal, that journey may take you somewhere that you did not expect to go, and that is fantastic. Just remember, you will never get anywhere if you stand still. In fact, the world will pass you by.

Movement forward requires focus. Do you want to be a fireman? Then focus on being the best fireman in the unit. Are you a teacher? Then focus on being the best teacher in your school system and inspiring kids to learn. Do you want to be a doctor? Focus on what it will take to be the best doctor that you can be. Do you dream about raising children? It's a noble endeavor that requires focus to be good.

Focus and Business

Focus is also important in the business world. One computer company has succeeded where others have failed because they focus on selling computers and computer equipment direct to the consumer. One airline has succeeded because they fly one plane, a 737 (creates efficiency in maintenance), in their own special way-- with cheap fares, fun service and on time. Would you buy shoes from the computer company or tacos from the airline? Another major company owns diverse businesses, but they achieved extraordinary results by focusing on core principles across all of those business units, including the goal of always being first or second in a business category.

Focus Your Days

Focus enters into the achievement of goals big and small. Losing twenty pounds requires focus. Improving your relationship with your spouse requires focus. Becoming the best salesperson in your company requires focus. Improving your grade point average requires focus. Becoming a more involved member of your church requires focus. The key is to make a decision. You can do it.

As focus is important in determining where our life is headed, it also plays a very important role in determining where our day is headed. Typically, our days are made up of many different tasks and responsibilities. Some of those tasks and responsibilities evolve from decisions that we make, and some are based on decisions that other people make for us. The question is whether we run and direct our days, or we let our responsibilities, tasks, outside influence, and the directions of others run us. People who are working to live wonderful lives and achieve their goals understand the importance of focus and establishing priorities in their daily lives.

Planning your day and setting daily priorities is an important part of success. Setting daily priorities determines where you will be placing your focus. Your priorities are determined by deciding which goals and tasks are the most important and immediate. Once you have established your priorities, planning the day determines how you will use your time to complete tasks and accomplish goals. In other words, it takes your focus down to the detail level. There are many products and seminars available today to help you with the prioritizing and planning of your life and your day. The Franklin-Covey system is an excellent example.

Visit an office supply store and you will see the shelves lined with day planners and forms to be used in planning and prioritizing. With all of the tools available to help with focus, organization and prioritization, it is incredible that so many people and businesses struggle with focus and organization. Finding the perfect system is not important. *Starting* the process of establishing priorities, learning about organizational skills and putting focus in your life is critical to your ultimate success. Once you begin, and if you remain focused on establishing priorities and planning, a system that works best for you will emerge. Make a decision and start the process.

You can do it.

It's Time To Focus

A manager walked up to her employee who was sitting in his cubicle workspace with papers stacked everywhere. She looked quizzically at the obviously flustered marketing coordinator and said "Tim, are you going to get the presentation done by 3pm?"

Tim looked up at his boss and with the exasperation of an overworked, tired "go to" person replied, "I'm not sure, I've got a lot on my plate right now."

This did not go over well. "Tim", chastised his frustrated boss, "You need to get focused."

Tim's reply echoes how many feel in today's busy, downsized world. "I plan to; I just don't have time right now. I have too much to do. Maybe next week."

The best advice for Tim is to start today. Next week too easily turns into next month. This too easily turns into next year, which too easily turns into "you're fired."

> *"Concentrate your energies, your thoughts and your capital..."*
> *-Andrew Carnegie*

Key to developing the attribute of focus is the determination to stay focused or your goal or ambition. This takes concentration, perseverance, tenacity, enthusiasm and courage. It is a terrific example of how the eight key attributes work together to help you create an extraordinary, wonderful life. Each and every day we are faced with challenges, distractions and obstacles that work to weaken or sidetrack our focus. We make progress on our goals when, despite the obstacles and distractions, we make consistent progress toward our ultimate desires.

Focus By The Pound

As an example of the difficulty that sometimes occurs when working to stay focused, take a battle that many of us have fought at least one time or another in our lives: losing weight. Once you have made the decision to lose weight, set your goal for how many pounds you intend to lose and pick a course of action (a diet, a plan for exercise, or both), the actual hard work begins. And so do the distractions.

Your boss calls an early morning meeting which throws off your exercise schedule. Oh well, you'll work out harder tomorrow. Then, your office decides to order stuffed pizza to celebrate a terrific month end. You want to be perceived as the team player that you are, so you skip your salad and walk at lunch. The pepperoni was excellent.

That evening, your top account has offered to take you and your boss out for drinks and dinner to thank you for all of your support on the big project. Of course you share dessert; it's a celebration! Because you got in late and you were not home to help with homework, your son has written you a note asking if you will get up early and help him with a story that he is writing for school. So, you'll skip tomorrow morning's workout and help your son. And then, at the end of the week, you step on the scale and wonder why your diet isn't working and you have gained half a pound.

If losing weight is important, then it is important to remain focused on the goal. How about waking up a half hour earlier and getting a modified workout in before the early meeting. When your co-workers order pizza, ask them to order a salad too. Celebrate with the team, but eat your way. At dinner, drink sparkling water and eat fish with vegetables. Then, have one spoonful of the dessert, not half. Help your son the next morning, and then ask him to go for a walk or run with you when you get home that evening. If you are focused on your goal, there are always practical solutions to the daily challenges.

> *"Paying attention to simple little things that most men neglect makes a few men rich."*
> *-Henry Ford*

There are two questions about focus that we get more than any others. First, is it possible to focus on more than one thing or goal? What if I want to be a great business owner and a great mother? The answer is a simple-

- yes. It is possible to have two areas of focus that are important to you. Many people, who live wonderful lives, achieve their dreams and make the lives of other people extraordinary do this. Here's the key to success: you will need to prioritize and focus your time and resource around those goals. There are activities and commitments that you will need to pass on. You will need to say no.

Another question we get deals with creativity. Some people are afraid that if they focus on one specific area in their lives or business, they won't have the freedom to explore, discover and be creative. Reality is quite the contrary. Focus actually allows for greater creativity and exploration because it provides a point of concentration for that creativity. Focus is the engine that can drive the creative mind.

Gene the Tire King

The attribute of focus is very powerful, especially when developed and used in combination with the other attributes. Take the story of Gene L.

After working years in the tire business for a major tire manufacturer, he and his partners bought a group of six tire stores in a Midwestern city. With their own money and the support of the Small Business Administration, they set up their business. Their focus was simple. They sold tires and they serviced cars, providing fair pricing and great service. Over the years, Gene L. and his partners built their business. Year after year they focused on their core business and focused on improving the service and value they provided. Twenty years later, their company has grown from those six initial stores to 23 retail locations, a wholesale tire division and over 200 employees.

Gene L.'s incredible success is based on his relentless focus, his courage and his absolute enthusiasm for his business. You have the ability to write the same kind of story for yourself. It is right there inside of you. You can do it.

You can develop and use the attribute of focus in your life. Here are three ideas.

Idea #1: Your Point of Focus on a 3x5 Card

Find a three by five index card and a pen. Can't find an index card? Make a three by five piece of paper. Next, go to a quiet place where you can sit and think without being interrupted. Once you have found this place, sit and think about all of your dreams, goals and ambitions. Now, pick one. Pick the one that you feel most passionately about. Write it down, in simple terms, on your index card. Next, write three brief reasons why this is important to you. Finally, write down two ways that you will work to realize your goal. This is your point of focus.

Carry this index card with you everywhere. Review it in the morning when you wake up. Review it at least once during the day. Review it at night before you go to sleep. Do this for thirty days. At the end of thirty days review your progress toward your goal. Repeat.

Idea #2: The Focus Journal

At the beginning of every day, take fifteen minutes to look at your priorities for that day. Where will you place your focus? Make decisions and move forward. At the end of each day, take fifteen minutes to write down the things you did and steps you took to act on those priorities. Keep the list short and focused. Do this for thirty days.

Idea #3: Develop a Statement of Belief or Credo

Companies and organizations all over the world write mission statements that guide their actions and plans. Some organizations spell out the values that their organization lives by each day. No matter the format, each serves the purpose of providing focus for those entities.

Individuals can undertake something similar by taking the time to write a personal credo or statement of belief. Start by listing the things that are important to you in life. Add to that your personal expectations for your attitude and behavior. In short, outline how you want to live your life. Don't worry about format. Focus on making the list to the point and complete. Then, put your statement of personal beliefs away.

After thirty days, review your statement. Evaluate your attitude, behavior and accomplishments against the statement. If revisions are necessary, make the changes. Use your statement to help give your life focus and clarity. Evaluate and rewrite your statement once a year.

Chapter 6

The Attribute of Urgency

"What you can do, or dream you can do, begin it; boldness has genius,
power and magic in it."
-Johann von Goethe

Definition
Urgency, n. 1. The quality or condition of being urgent; pressing importance.
2. A pressing necessity.

Synonyms
Importance, Necessity, Need, Exigency, Pressure, Stress, Hurry, Rush

Related Words/Phrases
Crisis Management, Critical Priority, Stat, ASAP, I needed it Yesterday.

There is a real difference between developing the attribute of urgency in your life, and living in the world of the urgent. Unfortunately, many of us spend most of our busy lives living in the world ruled by the urgent. The advancement of technology, which allows for instantaneous and always connected communication, combined with busy family schedules and pressure to perform in all aspects of life, has thrust many into living a culture of "need it yesterday".

Shannon's World of the Urgent

Shannon knows all about living in a life ruled by the urgent. As an assistant for the sales division of a major company, she coordinates presentation materials and phones for seven account executives, handles administrative assistant duties for two managers, and responds to customer emails on a daily basis. Two years ago, Shannon worked with five other assistants to handle the administrative duties of the department. Over the past two years, the number of assistants has dropped from six to two. The workload, however, has not decreased.

By 10:15a.m. one morning, Shannon had eleven internal emails from account executives and managers asking for help on projects that needed to be completed that day. All of the emails were sent with urgent notification, with apologies for short notice, and stressed the importance of the project. Also in her email inbox sat twenty emails from clients with questions.

No one would have been surprised if Shannon had taken her PDA, cell phone and laptop and thrown them in the dumpster on the way to lunch. Unfortunately, she didn't have time. She was to busy answering email to take lunch that day. The world of the urgent was running Shannon's life.

"We are always getting ready to live, but never living."
-Ralph Waldo Emerson

Shannon's story is shared by many in all walks of life. Many of us get so caught up living in the world of the urgent that we confuse this with developing the attribute of urgency. Interestingly enough, developing the attribute of urgency in combination with focus can keep us from getting bogged down in someone else's urgent world.

For years a major shoe company has encouraged action through their simple brand slogan. Their slogan is good advice, and it certainly has helped build one of the worlds most powerful brands. We would propose taking their statement a step further, creating a powerful brand slogan for the attribute of urgency.

Our statement for urgency is: Just do it, now. It is a clear message. Do you have something that you need or want to do? Start it. Do you have a dream you would like to pursue? Do it. You should approach each day with passion for getting things done. Do not procrastinate. Do not waste time. By developing the attribute of urgency, you can avoid the trap of living in others' urgent world.

> *Begin doing what you want to do **now**.*
> *-Marie Beynon Ray*

Shannon was unhappy living in her urgent world. She went to work unhappy, she left work unhappy, and she shared her unhappiness with her family at home. As you might imagine, she wasn't a real joy to be around. Her friends, co-workers and family started to cut a wide berth around Shannon. That is, of course, unless they needed something from her urgently. Then, they would just bear her unhappiness to get what they needed. The only person Shannon wasn't helping was herself.

From Urgent To Urgency

How can developing the attribute of urgency help Shannon to reclaim happiness, move away from living in the world of the urgent and move toward living a wonderful life? It is already apparent that Shannon was not happy with the current state of her life, because she was expressing unhappiness to everyone around her who would listen (and probably a few who wouldn't). Shannon needed to do something about her unhappiness, and she needed to start immediately, once she had made her decision.

At work, Shannon needed to take charge of her workload. By working with her team to develop a tool to communicate presentation timetables, she can begin streamlining her workload. A conversation with her supervisor detailing her workload and asking for guidance would be appropriate, given that many managers do not have a complete understanding of the impact of downsizing on the workforce. It's possible that some of the workload could be eliminated or shifted. Finally, if Shannon's peers and supervisors are unwilling to work with her, then she needs to make another decision. Shannon needs to change jobs or careers, or follow a dream.

As people who empathize with Shannon's plight, we anticipate that Shannon may feel that making a major change is impractical and unrealistic: there's not enough time in the day; it's hard to find a job; the situation may improve at the company and she would miss out; the grass isn't always greener… everything is the same at other companies; she needs the insurance. The list can go on, but the bottom line is the same. Most of the reasons that we give for inaction and not acting with urgency are based on our fear of the unknown, fear of change and in some cases, plain laziness. It is through thoughtful action driven by the attribute of urgency that we turn our fears into achievement.

"Courage to start and willingness to keep everlasting at it are the requirements for success."
-Alonzo Newton Benn

Our days will always contain projects and priorities that have a degree of urgency to them. That is inescapable. The attribute of focus helps in prioritizing and managing our "to do" list. The attribute of urgency provides the drive to get our "to do" list done. When we embrace the attribute of urgency, we embrace action.

Urgency dictates that we don't just show up to work, we show up to work hard. Urgency orders that we don't casually love when it's convenient; we love with all of our heart. Urgency states that when we see someone in need, we don't wait to see if someone else steps up to help; we lead the cause. The attribute of urgency prescribes that if we know are doing something that is harmful to us, that we stop right now.

The attribute of urgency does not negate thought and planning. It supports active thought and planning. As an example, let's refer back to Shannon. If Shannon woke up one morning and decided to quit her job that day because she hated it, without any thought for how to make money and put food on her families table, that would be irresponsible urgency. However, if Shannon decides to leave her job and begins immediately to plan an exit strategy and interview for other positions, that's responsible urgency. The key is to take action and move forward.

You really need to lose twenty pounds. Okay, make it thirty. You really need to complete your degree. You really need to spend more time with your children. You really need to brush up on your Power Point skills. You really need to improve your spiritual relationship. You really need to see that financial planner. You really need to call your mother. You really need to ask for a raise. Do any of these "you reallys" belong to you? Take action. Longfellow said, "Act... act in the living present." So what if they all belong to you. Sort them out, prioritize them, and check them off one by one.

Procrastinate and life will pass you by. Live with urgency, and you can live an extraordinary life and achieve your dreams. Here are three ideas that you can use to develop your attribute of urgency:

Idea #1: Get Started

The attribute of urgency is all about action. If you want to start something, take action. Remember our slogan? Just do it, now. So that's what you should do: start something.

Pick an activity, a goal or a project that you know you need to start, but you have been procrastinating. Take a sheet of paper and write down your action across the top.

For example, let's say that you want to lose twenty pounds, and you've decided that diet and exercise are your plan of attack. Don't wait until next week, or New Year's Day. Start today. For the next thirty days, take three minutes to record your daily progress. Write down what you eat and record your exercise. You can take this to the next level by developing a progress grid to follow. Here's a real-life example:

My Fitness Chart (Example)
Dedication, Determination and Discipline

Week→	8/28	9/4	9/11	9/18
Exercise	per workout	per workout	per workout	Per workout
Rotate Stretch	20x	20x	20x	20x
Side Stretch	20x	20x	20x	20x
Knee Bends	20x	20x	20x	20x
Crunch's	20x	30x	40x	40x
Legs Elev Crunch			10x	10x
Bicycle Cruch			10x	10x
Back Leg Push			10x each leg	10x each leg
Push-ups				20x

Walking Time	45min	45min	45min	45min
Walking Speed	1.4	1.5	1.6	1.6
Walking Incline	0	0	0	0
Freq. Of Exercise	4x	5x	4x	5x
Avg Weight	210	207	206	202

Keep your log for thirty days. You can do it.

Idea #2: Make a Promise

Has someone been encouraging you to take action in a particular way, perhaps to stop smoking? Make them a promise to take action, set a date in the near future, and then ask for their help and encouragement. Keep your promise and take action, and keep at it for at least thirty days. Reward yourself and your partner. Keep it up. You can do it!

Idea #3 The Urgency Quiz

Take the following quiz and be honest. How do you rate yourself? Ask someone close to you to rate you based on their observations. How do the two evaluations compare?

	Never		Always
When I have something important to do, I always take action.			
I respond to information by taking action on what I learn.			
I approach everything I do with energy and a will to get it done.			
I act before thinking.			
I keep promises.			

I have a long list of New Year's Resolutions every year.			
I consistently move items on my "to do" list from one day to the next.			
The people who get things done around me annoy me, the show offs.			

Are there any areas from the quiz where you can use some improvement? Pick one, and focus on improving in this area over the next thirty days.

You can do it!

Chapter 7

The Attribute of Perseverance

"Great works are performed not by strength, but by perseverance."
-Samuel Johnson

<u>Definition</u>
Perseverance, n. 1. The act of persevering; persistence in anything undertaken; persistent determination; continued pursuit of any enterprise begun.

<u>Synonyms</u>
Insistence, Resolve, Purposefulness, Steadfastness, Determination, Doggedness, Persistence, Tenacity, Constancy

<u>Related Words/Phrases</u>
Stick-to-itiveness, Endurance, Going the Extra Mile, Never Giving Up

Enthusiasm is the powerful attribute that allows us to see the opportunities that come from the obstacles we face. Perseverance is the powerful attribute that enables us to weather the storms that obstacles create on our way to opportunity.

If you are working to live an extraordinary life and achieve your dreams, you will face obstacles along the way. That is a given. Some of these obstacles can take the face of ridicule or doubt from those around you. You may face financial obstacles as you work to achieve your dream. People that you are close to may not support your dream because they fear change or the unknown.

In facing these obstacles, you will need to draw on the attributes of enthusiasm, courage and faith. With the purposefulness of a river cutting a canyon through rock, you will persevere and you will succeed.

James Madison, Abraham Lincoln, Thomas Edison, Mother Theresa, Henry Ford, Martin Luther King, Jr. and other inspirational leaders all faced tremendous obstacles as they followed their dreams and goals. They faced temporary setbacks, failures and oftentimes ridicule. Some even gave their lives in pursuit of their dream. Ultimately, they (or their dreams) persevered and contributed to the rich life that we enjoy today. What would our lives be like if courageous dreamers around us gave up at the first obstacle? Would you have the freedom to live your dream? Would you enjoy the freedom or resource to buy this book, or any book for that matter? We are so fortunate that others, through sacrifice and resolve, have inspired our dreams and given us the right to persevere in pursuit of our dreams.

"Energy and persistence conquer all things."
-Benjamin Franklin

The attribute of perseverance is not reserved for only a select few like the wealthy or the strong. It is inside each of us, waiting to be developed. It was inside a regular guy named Gene, and he utilized it on his way to achieving his dreams and living an extraordinary life.

Gene the Inventor

Gene M. grew up living the average American life. Gene M. lived in the same house for most of his youth, attended high school with the friends that he had grown up with, graduated and went right to work. No one had really encouraged Gene M. to attend college, so it made sense to go to work for McDonnell Douglas because he enjoyed working with his hands and designing things. A few years later, he got married to Sherl, and like many married couples, they bought their first home and began to raise a family.

Over time, Gene M. began to develop his engineering and design skills. He had talent, and it was recognized by people around him who encouraged him to pursue a degree in engineering. As he worked toward his degree, his talents were recognized inside the company and his responsibilities grew. At this point, you are probably expecting to learn that Gene M. is now the Chairman of an aerospace firm. No, not even close. It's better than that.

While working in a traditional setting, raising a family and attending school, Gene began to let his talent for design and engineering take a creative route as he experimented with invention. He started with little things. Then, he designed and built a small racing boat. He had thoughts of mass production, but that fell by the wayside. He dabbled with a few other things, always believing that he had the "big idea" inside of him.

One day, the idea struck. He would design a plastic cover for pickup truck beds that would compete with the fiberglass covers that were typically sold. It took him some time, but he finally came up with a design that not only met his rigorous demands, but also truly differentiated his product from any competitors.

He had the design and a sample product. Now came the hard part. Gene M. knew that to be successful, he had to sell his idea to a manufacturer. He took his design and idea on the road and met with obstacle after obstacle. He met with people who offered false promises. He met with companies who said yes all the way to the final meeting, and then said no. He met with companies who only took the meeting so that they could see his design.

"With ordinary talent and extraordinary perseverance, all things are attainable."
-Sir Thomas, Foxwell Buxton

From the very start and through the entire process Gene M. was met with challenges and obstacles. People told him he was wasting his time. He had financial obstacles. He had design obstacles. He even faced ridicule for pursuing his dream. Did he think of giving up? Sure, several times. The good news is that he didn't. Gene persevered. He eventually found a company who was willing to partner with him to launch the product. The company saw something in the design and cover that afforded them the courage to risk launching a new product.

As a result of his perseverance and experience, Gene M. learned incredibly powerful lessons that he applies today to his life and work. A man of strong faith, Gene M. glows in his achievement and yet remains humble with his blessings. What became of the truck bed cover that Gene M. brought to market using the attribute of perseverance? It is now the fastest- growing truck bed cover in America. That's the power of perseverance!

Nothing in the world can take the place of persistence. Talent will not; nothing is more common than unsuccessful individuals with talent. Genius will not; unrewarded genius is almost a proverb. Education will not; the world is full of educated derelicts. Persistence and determination alone are omnipotent."
-Calvin Coolidge

The attribute of perseverance is sitting inside waiting for you to develop it or improve on its use. It stands at the ready as you begin your first job and compete in the business world. It marches into battle with you as you begin that much anticipated weight loss program with urgency. It urges you on as you send manuscript after manuscript to publishers. It works with you as you try to communicate with your teenage daughter and protect her in a turbulent world. It pushes you as you work to repair a relationship that is on the brink of failure. It inspires you as you make the one hundredth revision on a design.

There is nothing easy about remaining steadfast in the face of difficulties. Throughout time, people have made tremendous sacrifice to persevere. Think of how many people have given their life to preserve freedom, or how many people have given their lives so that others may enjoy a better quality of life. For most of us, we will never experience sacrifices as great as those in the pursuit of our dreams, and we are very fortunate that there are brave men and woman who have been and will be willing to sacrifice everything for us.

There are people all around you, regular men and women just like us, who are living wonderful lives and achieving their dreams because they are developing the attribute of perseverance. The ability to persevere is inside of you. You can do it!

Here are three ideas for developing your attribute of perseverance:

Idea #1: Find a Persistent Mentor

You know that stubborn, persistent person who always seems to get what he desires (and often annoys you in the process)? Instead of avoiding them, seek them out. Talk to them about how they find the energy and strength to persevere. Ask them what they use as motivation to be persistent and how they avoid throwing in the towel. Study their behavior and model the traits that you feel comfortable using yourself. When you feel your persistence fading, seek their counsel and their support.

Idea #2 Persistently Pursue a Goal

In Chapter 6 you were encouraged to begin something that you have been putting off-- the pursuit of a goal or dream. For this idea, we encourage you to tie your development of perseverance to this goal. During the thirty day period when you are working on your goal, write down your thoughts about your progress on a daily basis. After thirty days, review your notes. Did you ever feel like quitting? What happened to make you feel that way? What did you do to convince yourself to move forward? Learn from your experience and use it in the future.

Idea #3: The Three Minute Power Talk

This isn't chanting, meditation or self hypnosis. It is actually a form of visualization. It may sound silly, but give it a try; it really works. At some point during your day, take three minutes for yourself and find a place without distraction. Describe something to yourself that you are working to achieve or trying to accomplish. Remind yourself that you are doing this so that you can live a wonderful life and achieve your dreams. Finish your power talk with the statement: "I can do this. I will succeed." You will be doing the same thing that many professional athletes and successful people do on a daily basis, and you will be working to develop your attribute of perseverance.

Chapter 8

The Attribute of Courage

"Courage is the most important of all virtues, because without it we can't practice any other virtue with consistency."
-Maya Angelou

Definition
Courage, n. 1. The state or quality of mind or spirit that enables one to face danger, fear, or vicissitudes with self-possession, confidence and resolution; bravery.

Synonyms
Bravery, Guts, Nerve, Valor, Daring, Audacity, Fortitude, Heroism

Related Words/Phrases
Power, Daring, Grit, Show No Fear

It was a small sailboat, the kind that you can sail off a beach or on a small lake. The catamaran was a perfect boat for the inexperienced sailors. With one sail, two pontoons and a canvas deck it offered speed and a chance to get away from the noise and pressure of everyday life. It wasn't as fancy as some of the other boats on the beach, but it was theirs, and that's all that mattered.

As they grew more experienced at sailing, they would push themselves and test their skills. They would sail out further into the lake, to the point that the people on the beach were little specks. When it was windy, they would tighten the sail so that the boat would rise up on one pontoon. They would sail along until a gust would push the boat over so that it rested on one pontoon and its wild occupants were thrown into the water. They would laugh at themselves, right the boat as they had learned, and continue on their journey.

The best ride always occurred right before a storm blew in. The wind would pick up and blow hard at a constant speed. The little boat would move quickly through the water, the tight mast humming against the strain of the gusts. The sound of the hum was exhilarating. They never missed an opportunity to make the sail hum.

One afternoon they sailed off the beach more excited than usual. It was a beautiful day, with no sign of storms, and yet the wind was blowing hard and strong. The sail would hum that day for sure. As they sailed out into the big lake, they took advantage of the strong wind to move quickly off shore. The wind did not let them down, and the sail hummed.

What happened next was something for which neither one of them was prepared. A sudden powerful gust pushed the sail over and threw them both into the water. Instead of lying upright on one pontoon as the boat had always done, a portion of the mast broke and flipped the boat completely over.

Father and son came up out of the ice cold water sputtering. Both men had been hit by the boat as it toppled over, but fortunately they both had life jackets on and came to the surface quickly. Fear gripped the son. At first, he could not see or hear his father, and he had lost his bearings. Then in the next second he heard his father calling his name. "Are you all right?" came the yell simultaneously from father and son. They swam around the boat to find each other and get a handle on their predicament. They worked for a minute to try and right the boat, but quickly realized that their efforts were useless. The strong wind and heavy mast would make it impossible. The son tried not to show his fear, but it was starting to take over his thoughts. They were stranded, with no way to signal for help, in very cold and very deep water.

The father knew that they were in a tough predicament, and that his son was growing more afraid by the moment. He swam next to his son. This situation called for courage; courage that he would have to find and share. He reassured his son that the boat could not sink, and that if they kept their heads and their lifejackets on, they would not sink either. And then, with great courage, he looked his son in the eye and said, "I will not let anything happen to you son. I promise." The strength and courage in his father's voice reassured the son and together they worked to paddle the boat toward the shore. After a short time, in answer to a prayer, a huge cabin cruiser stopped and offered assistance. The small sailboat was towed to the shore, and the adventurous sailors were returned to the firm ground.

"Courage is the first of human qualities because it is the quality which guarantees all others."
-Sir Winston Churchill

When we think of stories of courage, our minds flash to stories of famous sports figures, wartime generals or historical leaders whose images of bravery have been told to us in movies and books. Truth be told, ordinary men and women exhibit profound courage every day. There's the woman who bravely fights breast cancer, yet continues to work and care for her family; the doctor who risks his own life to fight disease in a third world country; the young man, guided by his heart, who travels the street at night searching for homeless teenagers and children who need shelter; the fireman who rushes into a burning building to save a human life, not knowing if he will be able to make it out alive; the person of faith who reaches out to others in a spiritual sense, risking ridicule; the teacher who has a passion for teaching and works with children in the inner city; the soldier who fights for freedom, knowing the unseen enemy may be waiting in ambush; the teenager who does not take a drink from a friend at a party.

Fear is a common human emotion that we first experience as children and carry with us in different forms throughout our lives. Fear is natural, and can sometimes serve us well by keeping us from danger. For example, taking shelter during a storm is a smart thing to do and is driven by our fear of harm, based on the knowledge of what a severe storm can do. Courage does not mean that fear is not present. Courage exists with the knowledge of fear, and the determination to prevail in spite of it. Mark Twain said it well: "Courage is resistance to fear, mastery of fear- not absence of fear."

Courage on Display

Ordinary people summon courage in the darkest of hours, despite fear. As an example, one day a terrible car accident occurred as a family was traveling. The occupants of the car were tossed about and as the mangled car came to rest, their horrific injuries came to light. Despite a severe head injury, the man had the presence of mind and courage to exit the car and insure the safety of his loved ones. It was only then that he collapsed into a coma. The woman, who was knocked unconscious, woke up to insure that her small children were safe, keeping them at her side despite a broken back and severe injuries that immobilized her. Both of them displayed remarkable courage, neglecting themselves for the protection and safety of others.

We don't see courage only through public displays of bravery. Courage often occurs in the quiet of our thoughts and heart. It is a business person's quiet decision to stand with integrity and not profit from the unethical; it is the parent's quiet determination to not drink or smoke after their child has gone to bed; it is the writer's determination to question popular thinking; it is the child's decision not to look up the answers to the problems when they are in the back of the book; it is the dreamer's quest to hold on to his ideas in the face of ridicule; it is the man's decision to get help in controlling his fear of leaving his house; it is the decision of a woman to leave her abusive husband; it is the decision of a teenager to pursue higher education when friends and family don't encourage it. Quiet acts of courage like these are undertaken every day in our world. They fuel our growth as a society and softly inspire others to make courageous decisions.

"Courage and perseverance have a magical talisman, before which difficulties disappear, and obstacles vanish into air."
-John Quincy Adams

As you work to develop the eight important attributes discussed in this book, you will find that courage is interwoven into all of them. Living a wonderful life and achieving dreams takes courage. By making a decision to live a wonderful life, you are moving away from the ordinary; you are saying that you are not content to live in and with mediocrity. You are going to work to make your life and the lives of those around you extraordinary. Guess what? You are going to ruffle some feathers. Have courage and persevere-- you can do it! Ultimately, those around you will benefit from the mark that you make.

We have been given wonderful gifts: the gift of thought, the gift of speech, the gift of imagination and the gift of physical movement to name a few. The extraordinary nature of these gifts places upon us a responsibility to use them to our fullest potential. We are not entitled to live a wonderful life, but our gifts allow for it. The understanding of the significance of these gifts and the courage to use them to live our own extraordinary life is inside each of us. We only have to learn to develop our attributes, and have the courage to act. You can do it.

Here are three ideas that you can use to develop the attribute of courage:

Idea #1: Work Through a Fear

Have you seen the network television show where people take on their worst fears? People compete by conquering their fears and experiencing sometimes horrific stunts, like being covered with cockroaches. Watching the show, we don't think that those people are necessarily brave, we think they're crazy. Nonetheless, you can participate in your own, much more civilized and sane version of the show on a personal level.

Take something that makes you nervous. For example, many people are intimidated and fearful of public speaking. Set up a challenge for yourself, with a reward for completion. Get a book or videotape with advice for new or fearful public speakers. Once read (or viewed) write a three-minute speech on any topic you choose. Practice it three times in front of the mirror before your toughest critic-- you. Then, gather just a few friends or family members together and present your three-minute speech. Make sure these are people that you trust and people that you can laugh with. If you need to, imagine them in their underwear. Well, all except Grandpa John. Finish your speech and enjoy your gallon of ice cream. You can choose to tackle a different fear, just make sure to follow the same principle of practice, experience and reward.

Idea #2: Study Brave People

We can learn a great deal about courage by studying history. Find information or stories about one or two courageous people. Learn as much as you can about their courageous acts. Take time to think and put yourself in their position. How would you respond to the challenges they faced? What do your share in common with these people?

Idea #3 Help Someone Else Find Courage

There are people all around us who are less fortunate, or who face battles that are much more significant than ours. There are some people who are in desperate need of courage just to live another day. Seek out people in need by volunteering through your church or a civic organization. Offer them comfort and support. By sharing yourself with others, you may give them the help they need to summon courage and face their own problems. Their courage will inspire you to do the same.

Chapter 9

The Attribute of Faith

"Faith is the daring of the soul to go farther than it can see."
-William Newton Clark

<u>Definition</u>
Faith, n. 1. Confident belief in the truth, value or trustworthiness of a person, idea, or thing 2. Belief that does not rest on logical proof or material evidence 3. Loyalty to a person or thing; allegiance 3. the theological virtue defined as secure belief in God and a trusting acceptance of God's will. 5. The body of dogma of a religion. 6. A set of principles or beliefs.

<u>Synonyms</u>
Confidence, Trust, Reliance, Assurance, Conviction, Belief, Devotion, Commitment

<u>Related Words/Phrases</u>
Unwavering Belief, Credo, Truth

At one time or another, each of us has had our back against the wall, faced with a challenge or obstacle that would appear insurmountable to an outsider. And yet somehow, deep down in the core of our being, we knew that the situation would work out and that everything would turn out okay.

We held on to that belief as we worked through our issues, emerging on the other side having tackled the problem and succeeded. Our belief that the situation would turn out may have been centered on our faith in God and his leading to an answer. It may have rested in our trust of another human being and the faith that they would help us prevail. We may have even had deep-seated faith in our own abilities based on past experience and courage.

It is deep-seated belief, an assurance from our very soul, which constitutes faith. Faith is the attribute that sparks hope. Faith fosters courage and lights enthusiasm. It can be knowledge that defies what our senses bring us in terms of information, and faith can be the torch that lights our way through the darkness of difficult times. Faith is encouragement; our friends and colleagues will urge us on with cries of "Keep the faith," and "Don't lose faith." Faith can be comfort in our darkest hours.

A minister in the heat of a sermon was once overheard telling his church that "Faith is concrete, you either have it or you don't." To him, faith was absolute; an issue of contrasting colors. With all due respect to the minister, because faith is a journey, there are definite shades of grey. Our journey is what ultimately carries us to the point where we have faith that we can live a wonderful life and achieve our dreams.

"Faith is to believe what you do not yet see; the reward for this faith is to see what you believe."
-Saint Augustine

When we are born, we are an open canvas ready to be painted with life experience. As a small child, we have enormous faith in many things, and exhibit our faith with tremendous enthusiasm. Our world is comprised of what we are taught and what we find in exploration. Then, as we enter the age of reason, our childlike blind faith begins to erode. We begin to question everything, especially the things that we can't see, feel, touch or experience. As we mature, we begin to understand that there are truths and principles beyond our reason which many hold dear, and we begin to recognize the attribute of faith.

Faith's journey can be very rocky. Our faith can be tested by the loss of a loved one, or a long debilitating struggle. Our faith in ourselves can be tested when we meet an obstacle that we just can't seem to overcome. Our faith in those we love can be tested when they disappoint us or fail to keep a promise. In our hearts, we always want to keep our faith. Our minds, however, can work against our keeping faith. When our faith is challenged, the key is to stay focused and patient.

"The only limit to our realization of tomorrow will be our doubts of today. Let us move forward with strong and active faith."
-*Franklin Delano Roosevelt*

You cannot buy faith. It is not bottled, canned or packed in a nice box with bubble wrap. You can't borrow your friends' faith, use it and return it one month later with their scissors. You can't pretend that you have faith, although many try, because pretend faith has no value. You can't download faith from the Internet, even if you have a high speed cable modem. You can't win faith in a sweepstakes, or claim it with a lottery ticket.

The Power of Faith and Love

The attribute of faith has the power to work everyday, extraordinary miracles. It was at the cornerstone of a miraculous recovery for a husband and a wife who lay gravely ill in separate hospitals. Each one had life-threatening injuries, the husband in a deep coma, the wife fading in and out of pain-racked consciousness.

Over the course of a week, the wife would ask for her husband, wanting to speak with him and find out about his condition. Each time she asked, she was only given a little information. She was not told that her husband lay in a life-threatening coma, and that doctors were losing hope for his ultimate survival. Finally, after one week of asking, the wife insisted that she be allowed to speak with her husband. She was told that he may not be able to respond, but she insisted nonetheless.

Family members held phones to each of their ears as the woman spoke to her husband. "Honey, can you hear me?" asked the wife. There was a pause, as she summoned the courage to ask again. "Honey, it's me. Can you hear me?" she asked again. Faith answered. The husband spoke his wife's name. Family members and nurses on both ends sobbed with joy. The wife asked, "Are you okay?" The husband answered, "Yes, I'm fine." Both husband and wife began the road to recovery.

Faith comes from deep, personal relationships. Spiritually, it comes from a deep, personal relationship with God. Emotionally, it comes from a deep personal relationship with those we love. And, it comes from deep personal knowledge of ourselves, our strengths and our limitations. Faith comes from hard work, meaningful experience, understanding and witnessing joy in others.

People who live wonderful lives work at growing their faith. They understand that faith is a journey and that their experiences will only help them to develop deeper faith if they stay patient and focused. It takes courage to have faith.

Too often, we tiptoe around the attribute of faith when discussing success and achievement. It might be based on the fear of mixing the spiritual and secular worlds. It might stem from a lack of understanding about the nature and power of faith. The truth is that any time that dreams, goals, success and achievement are involved, faith is at the core.

We have inside of each of us the ability to exercise and grow our attribute of faith. Faith is a gift that we control; it is a powerful attribute at our disposal.

Develop your faith and reap the rewards. You can do it!

Here are three ideas for developing the attribute of faith:

Idea #1: Develop Faithful Friends

One of the best ways to develop a skill or attribute is to surround yourself with people who exhibit the behavior or quality that you seek. This is a terrific way to develop faith! Surround yourself with people who have strong faith and conviction and demonstrate faith consistently. We are not suggesting that you insulate yourself. People who have developed a strong attribute of faith come in all shapes, sizes, races and genders. By observing their behavior and talking with them about their source of faith, you can learn to develop and grow your own.

Idea #2: Read About The Attribute of Faith

Learning plays an important role in the development and improvement of a quality or skill. A person playing the game of basketball improves his skills through practice and learning about the game. The same is true for golf. Improving and developing a personal attribute is no different. To learn more, read what others have to say. A good place to start is the local bookstore. Authors to investigate include John Maxwell, Stephen Covey, Napoleon Hill, Norman Vincent Peale, and Jack Canfield/Mark Victor Hansen.

Idea #3: The One Thing

Did you ever see the movie *City Slickers?* In the movie, the character Mitch (played by Billy Crystal) and his friends take a cattle driving vacation. During the trip, they meet Curly (played by Jack Palance) who sends them on a quest to figure out "the one thing" that matters in life. Each one of us has "the one thing" in which we have faith. What's yours? What drives your faith in the one thing? What can you learn from your faith in this one thing to develop and improve faith in other aspects of your life?

Chapter 10

The Attribute of a Sense of Humor

"Laugh loudly, laugh often, and laugh at yourself."
-Richard E. Rogala, PhD

<u>Definition</u>
Sense of Humor, n. 1. The trait of appreciating and being able to express the humorous.

Humorous, n. 1. Full of or characterized by humor; funny. 2. Employing or showing humor; witty.

<u>Synonyms</u>
Amusing, Comical, Whimsical, Witty, Pleasant, Merry

<u>Related Words/Phrases</u>
Side Splitting, LOL (Laugh Out Loud), Crack Up

We believe in the power of humor. Humor has the ability to heal, to inspire and to teach. Humor can increase the effectiveness of communication and can brighten the darkest of situations. Given the influence of this attribute, it is surprising that humor's important role in business, leadership and life is not written about more or taught in school. Many researchers have pointed to the fact that a sense of humor is one of the key qualities of successful business people and people in leadership roles. Humor is also touted as enhancing a person's mental well-being and social status.

Jeanne Robertson wrote a fantastic book about developing a sense of humor. In her book *Humor: The Magic of Genie. Seven Potions for Developing a Sense of Humor,* Robertson outlines the framework for her philosophy on humor: she believes that a sense of humor is one of the most important assets a person can possess; she thinks that being funny does not necessarily mean that a person has a sense of humor-- a sense of humor is simply a lifestyle; she believes that a good sense of humor can be developed and that desire, determination, and a little direction are the only necessary requirements for developing the attribute; finally, she believes that our actions can influence the people around us to develop or keep their sense of humor.[1]

The Wild Ride

Have you ever had the experience of facing a difficult situation and having humor provide comfort and perspective? It happened for one airline traveler who turned a wild ride into an antidote for relaxation.

Our traveler was returning home after a long business trip and a lengthy airport delay due to stormy weather at his home airport. He took comfort in the fact that he was upgraded to first class on the small, older jet as he settled in to his seat. Just when he thought that peace and quiet would be his for the next hour, two business associates boarded the plane and sat down in the row in front of him.

It was obvious that the two jovial men had spent their time celebrating a long wait at the airport bar. Their loud, raucous laughter filled the entire plane, their slightly slurred speech evidence of earlier merriment. As there were just two rows in this section of the plane, escaping their noise was impossible.

The noise grew as the flight progressed and the celebration continued. Flight attendants and other passengers grew increasingly weary of the fun-loving noise makers.

About twenty minutes before the end of the flight, the disruptive merriment stopped. Storms were still in the area of the travelers' destination, and the jet began to move around in the wind. As the plane began its decent, the pilot came over the speakers to tell the flight attendant to be seated and for the passengers to expect a rough ride. The plane fell silent as they rolled through the nighttime air. Lightning flashed all around as hands gripped armrests and seatbelts were tightened. At one point, the plane rolled violently to the right, causing the now silent, half-baked front seat passengers to let out a groan of pain. Our traveler knew they had to be close to landing, but it was impossible to tell where the plane was in relationship to the airport.

Suddenly, as the plane continued its quick descent, a loud mechanical voice coming from the cockpit broke the silence of the first class cabin. "Terrain! Terrain! Terrain!" the mechanical voice yelled. "That can't be good," thought our passenger as his thoughts were confirmed by the face of the airline attendant sitting outside the cockpit door facing the cabin. Terrain meant ground, and ground and flying planes don't mix well. (A side note: the mechanical voice was coming from the airplanes computerized ground detection unit, which is usually shut off at landing; apparently, in working to land the plane, it was not switched off by the co-pilot). As one voice from the cockpit stopped, another even more urgent, terrified voice came from one of the drunken passengers in the front seat: "Who the hell is Elaine and what is the captain doing with her in the cockpit???" came the slurred question.

There was a split second of silence, and then a whole section of the airplane erupted in the laughter of emotional release. In the next seconds, the plan landed safely, and as it rolled toward the terminal, the laughter continued. In fact, as our traveler left the baggage area, he could still here laughter coming from his fellow passengers.

From that point forward, each and every time a flight got rough and he felt the tension building, he would repeat these words to himself: "Who the heck is Elaine?" A smile would creep over his face and he would laugh quietly as the humor of everyday life helped him to relax.

> *"The most important ingredient in developing a sense of humor is being able to laugh at yourself."*
> *-Jeanne Robertson*

The ability to laugh at oneself is important. Gascoigne said, "An error gracefully acknowledged is a victory won. To make mistakes is human; to stumble is commonplace; to be able to laugh at yourself is maturity." We often look at those people who can't laugh at themselves and remark,

---

[1] From Humor: The Magic of Genie 1989 Rich Publishing Company.

"Well, that person has no sense of humor." Laughing at our own mistakes is something that people will notice-- if you do, and if you don't.

Have you ever sat through a presentation or a speech that was bone dry, with absolutely no wit or humor attached? Did you ever have a teacher that was devoid of a sense of humor? You probably don't remember much from those moments in time because, frankly, watching paint dry is not an inspiring activity. Not much is learned when counting head nods and snorts from those falling asleep is the only stimulation to the experience.

Work to add humor to your daily life, to your presentations and to your conversations. People who live wonderful lives and achieve their dreams understand that developing a sense of humor is critical to their ultimate happiness and success. You can do it!

We wholeheartedly suggest that you learn more about developing your sense of humor by seeking out Jeanne Robertson's book *Humor: The Magic of Genie*. Here are three suggestions for developing your sense of humor that come from her book:

Idea #1: Look For Humor in Everyday Situations

Jeanne suggests that we look for humor in our everyday lives by adding finding humor to our "to do" list; asking ourselves questions that lead to finding humor; asking our friends and acquaintances for humor; and by working with a humor buddy.

Idea #2: Associate with People Who Have a Sense of Humor

Similar to our idea offered with regard to associating with people who exhibit faith, the same applies for humor. This doesn't mean to head to the local comedy club and try to hang out with your favorite stand up comedian. It does mean to build relationships with people close to you who also value the attribute of a sense of humor. Work with that person on the development of your attribute and share humor whenever you can with that person.

Idea #3: Collect Humor

Humor is all around us. We experience humorous situations every day that make us laugh. They could be stories, jokes that friends told us, observations we've made about our behavior or other people's behavior.

The key is to collect them: write them down; put them in a file; keep them handy. Add to the collection whenever you experience humor. Jeanne writes that "taking a humor break each day with your humor cues (collection) is an important step in developing a sense of humor."[2]

Part III
Harness The Power of FUEL
In Your Life!

[2] Humor: The Power of Genie. 1989 Rich Publishing Co.

Chapter 11

The Letter and The Decision

"Man does not simply exist, but always decides what his existence will be, what he will become in the next moment."
-Viktor Frankel

The young freshman in high school was lying on the floor in the room of their house that was called "Dad's Study." It was an office of sorts, serving double duty as the family room, TV room and sun porch. This was the room where all of the important conversations took place, and this was an important conversation.

He had just brought home an interim report card that was, to say the least, not "satisfactory." The grades that the mother and father were staring at were not typical for their son. All through middle school and junior high, their son had achieved "A's" in all his classes, receiving awards and honors. Now, in his second semester of high school, they were looking at a few B's, a few C's, and a D- that looked perilously close to an F. Surely he was capable of more, which is what they explained patiently to him as he lay moping.

"Perhaps you overextended yourself,'" they offered.

"You seem to have trouble focusing," they suggested.

"You are capable of so much more," they counseled.

"We'll help you in every way that we can," they said, "but ultimately you will have to take responsibility for yourself. You will need to make this happen."

They just didn't understand. "You'll have to face it," the emotional young man sighed. "I'm just a C student. That's the best that I can do."

Fortunately, the parents were thoughtful, patient, and kinder than many people in the same circumstance would have been. However, they were also firm. The father spoke. "If that's what you believe, then you're entitled to your opinion. However, your life is going to change. From this point forward, as a C student, you will have the privileges and live the life of a C student." He then proceeded to outline the changes in life that the freshman would endure, and they were significant.

As so many conversations with teenagers end, this one ended the same way. There was the typical brooding, skulking off, moaning about an unfair life and hiding in the room. The parents were undeterred and the teenager was left to think through his situation.

Final report cards were due in three weeks, and the teenager abided by his new rules quietly. His mother and father waited patiently, knowing that their son was dealing with many thoughts and emotions.

On the evening before quarterly report cards were to come out, they found a sealed envelope on their bed addressed to them. It contained a hand written note on standard loose leaf notebook paper. Here is the content of that letter, in its entirety:

Dear Parents:

I don't think your son is going to do very well on his report card this quarter. In fact, I know I'm not. I guess you could say it's a show of a lack of responsibility! And, if you said that, you'd be right.

I guess I am still overwhelmed by the fact that this is high school. I guess I just can't say 'This is the big time now fella. Settle down and do some work.' I don't know what it is. I am disorganized and completely befuddled. I don't know why I am writing this instead of saying it to your face. I guess I feel better writing.

I am ashamed of myself. I guess I have to take high school more seriously. I am a big farto. If you only could see how ashamed of myself I am. I guess you could say I've opened my eyes to life.

But I know it's not your job to bail me out. Like you said, I have to do this myself. I need your help. Mom: If you would, would you get me six folders and an assignment book? Please! The folders should have pockets. I will write down all of my assignments for the day so I will remember them. And, will you please check all of my homework for the night so I won't slough off and say 'Aw, I'll do it tomorrow.' Maybe if you let me teach you what I learned it would be better.

Finally, please don't say anything or give me a lecture about this letter. I am now man enough to realize my own mistakes and take care of them. And, please don't let my sister know what an ass I am. And, when my report card comes, please don't give me a lecture on what I should do. I know what I have to do.

Please, with your help, I know I can do it. Things will work out.

Love,

Your Son

As it happened, things did work out. The mother bought the six pocket folders *and* the assignment notebook. No one gave lectures about the letter, or the report card that followed (not that there were not other times during the wonderful teenage years where lectures were deserved and delivered). The freshman worked hard, and his parents checked his homework every night.

Three years later, the "C" student graduated with honors, awards, and a grade point average that was well above his self proclaimed "C" level. With the love and support of his parents (and his sister who always knew he was a goofball but was kind enough not to tell him) he made a decision to turn a tough situation around. He worked hard. He succeeded.

We are all presented with decisions that affect the quality, richness and circumstances of our lives. There are times when we have people around us to provide encouragement and support through the decisions; and there are times when we are faced with making decisions when the only voices we hear are those of our thoughts and our soul. Ultimately, in either case, we must bare the full responsibility for the decisions that we make. It is our choice, and our choice alone, to decide to live a wonderful life, achieve our dreams, and make the lives of those around us extraordinary. The terrific news is that each of us has the ability to make that choice.

At the beginning of our discussion, we promised that we would only ask you to make two decisions. It is time for that second decision.

Do you desire a richness of life that brings you joy, happiness, comfort and success? Do you wish to live a wonderful life and achieve dreams that you never thought possible to achieve? Do you wish to make your life and the lives of those around your extraordinary? If so, then make your decision to start the process today. You alone can make that decision. A life of rich rewards stands in front of you. You can do it!

You hold the guideposts to living an extraordinary life and achieving your dreams in your hands. There are no quick fixes or cosmetic cover ups. The answers are right in front of you and the decision is yours. By working to develop these eight significant attributes, you can plot a course for terrific days and a wonderful life. It is understood that there will be stumbling blocks, risk and failure along the way. Your patience will be tested and your faith challenged. However, by committing to constant improvement and working slowly but surely to develop these attributes, you will attain your goal. As Will Rogers said "Even if you are on the right track, you'll get run over if you just sit there." Constant improvement is an important part of your growth.

What is it that you want to achieve? Do you want to start your own business? Do you want to lose twenty pounds? Do you want to repair and grow a relationship? Do you want to increase your sales? Do you want to make your classroom and teaching more meaningful and exciting? Do you want to develop a better relationship with your teenage daughter? Do you want to get a better job? Make your decision, commit to constant improvement, and with hard work your dreams will become reality.

You may question the long-term viability of your decision and commitment to live a wonderful life. Sometimes, we have difficulty looking past the next week much less five or ten years from now. How do you know that the decision you make today will truly make a difference in the long term? We can only answer by providing an example.

The Second Letter

Twenty years after his turbulent freshman year and the decision he made to begin using these eight attributes as his guidepost, our freshman (now dad and business person) received an envelope mailed by his parents. When he opened it, he found a copy of his original handwritten note attached to another handwritten note from his parents. Here is the content of that note:

Our Dear Son:
Dad and I were going through cards and memory stuff on Sunday
and we ran across this. As I read it out loud to Dad, he and I
both started to laugh and cry at the same time. Then we talked
about sending you a copy for you to look at and reflect on how

far you have come since freshman year of high school. But, more importantly we wanted to tell you how proud we are of you and the man you have become.

As you read this remember you have a little son and daughter that will probably be expressing these same sentiments to you someday. Be patient, kind and understanding, but firm in your knowledge that they too can do it if they try. I hope we weren't too hard on you in those days. You just needed a little help and encouragement over one of life's humps. You made it then and you will make it again. We know!

We love you very much.

The decision that young freshman made affected his life for the next twenty years, and years beyond that. Sure he came across obstacles, suffered setbacks and experienced failure. Through it all he has lived a wonderful life and achieved success beyond the imagination of any young teenager, and it all ties back to making that decision. It's the same decision you can make.

You can do it!

Chapter 12

FUEL for Your Life

"Energy and persistence conquer all things."
-Benjamin Franklin

The eight key attributes discussed in the previous chapters are potent by themselves; they are extremely powerful when brought together and harnessed by the human spirit in the desire to grow and succeed. These same principles can be harnessed by organizations determined to grow and prosper.

As you work to develop each attribute, you will find yourself also developing and growing others. For example, focus and urgency work together as you establish priorities and make decisions to act. Enthusiasm, courage and faith are all integral ingredients in the development of perseverance. Communication, sense of humor and enthusiasm are all ingredients in motivating others and making other people's lives extraordinary. All of the attributes, working together, are fuel for your life and fuel for your business.

Lists are difficult to remember, and in today's busy world, we certainly have a long list of things to remember. We want to make the list of powerful attributes something that you can easily remember and use as you make important decisions and work to make your life and the lives of people around you extraordinary.

Remember the acronym FUEL, and use it to drive success in your life:

       Focus
       Urgency
       Enthusiasm
       Leadership
            Positive Communication
            Perseverance
            Courage
            Faith
            Sense of Humor

When you apply FUEL to your life, you will create positive change. The attributes of Focus, Urgency and Enthusiasm in combination with the Leadership traits of Positive Communication, Perseverance, Courage, Faith and a Sense of Humor proactively developed will empower your success. These are your traits to use. You have ownership. You can apply them to your life. It's your decision.

The Young Salesperson Revisited

Do you remember the young salesperson from Chapter 2 who was ridiculed for being too enthusiastic? He stayed the course and remained enthusiastic, succeeding in the end.

Now, here's the rest of the story.

At some point in the process, the young account executive made a decision. He certainly felt the pressure from his peers to tone down his enthusiasm. In a candid conversation, he expressed frustration that his personality, which in the past had drawn people to him, was pushing people away. He was faced with two choices: he could pack his bags and move on, or he could work to improve his relationships and his work environment.

After careful thought, he came to the conclusion that he liked what he was doing and wanted to grow, so he made the decision to harness the FUEL attributes to improve his life. The decision was made (urgency) and he moved forward. He decided to concentrate (focus) on getting to know his co-workers better and center his conversations on their interests (communication). He decided to maintain his positive nature and love of life (enthusiasm), but worked to tone down his raucous laugh and volume (communication). He remained steadfast in his goal (perseverance), working to improve his relationships with his co-workers despite their resistance (courage, faith). Interestingly enough, with a quieter tone, his co-workers began to respond to his humorous insights and observations (sense of humor).

During this process, he came across another challenge. A position opened up in the management ranks of the company, and he decided to apply for the job. To his great disappointment, he was not promoted. Although he did not offer him the job, his manager did offer him an opportunity. He laid out a list of goals for the young salesperson. The manager offered his help, and committed that if the young salesperson met the established goals, he would move into a management job within one year. It was time for another decision, and once again he decided to harness the FUEL attributes. Within six months he had achieved the goals that had been established, and within nine months he was promoted, long before one year was up.

Over the years, that young salesperson remained committed to the eight key attributes. He faced challenges, obstacles and failures along the way. They never stopped him. Today, as president of an organization, he is living a wonderful life and continuing to achieve success beyond his dreams. Most significantly, he has made the lives of hundreds of people extraordinary because of his enthusiasm for life and his desire to see other people succeed.

A rich and rewarding life is within your reach. A strong and successful business is readily attainable. You can live an extraordinary life and achieve all of your dreams.

Make your decision. Put the FUEL attributes to work for you.

You can do it.

Acknowledgments

With heartfelt thanks and appreciation, the authors gratefully acknowledge:

Sharon and Mary... thanks for loving us and for your support, courage, partnership. Thanks for supporting starry-eyed dreamers as they follow their dreams. We will love you forever.

Nancy (Little Peach/Nooch)... you are a wonderful editor... and the sweetest, kindest, best, most amazing daughter and sister in the world. Someday, we hope to write as well as you...

Bryan and Lauren... I love you both. Words cannot describe the joy that you bring to my life, and how proud I am to be your father. Thank you for your editing and for your inspiration. The two of you and Mom are the fuel of my life.

Ron... there will never be a better big brother.

Steve, Stevie Ray and Allison... thank you for your love and support. Words can not describe the joy that you brought Poppy...

Dad L., Grandma, Gene, Sherl, Amanda and Erin... thanks for the inspiration and for your love.

Doug… here's to friendship and a great partnership; past, present and future.

Bruce H… thanks for the help, guidance and inspiration.

Pea Pod… thanks for the encouragement and friendship.

L and K… your insightful comments helped to craft a better message. Thanks for believing…

O… your feedback is invaluable and priceless.

M… thanks for proofing with enthusiasm and perseverance!

Sister Mary William… you believed, you guided and you loved. You are a hero to many… and a gift from heaven to us.

Mike… thanks for being my best friend and for teaching me so much about success and perseverance.

Dan… thanks for teaching me about importance, relevance and urgency… and for the wonderful friendship.

Thank you to the teams in St. Louis, Dallas, Pittsburgh, Grand Rapids, Cincinnati, Tampa and Indianapolis… I am honored to have worked beside you and grateful for your friendship.

About The Authors

Richard E. Rogala, Ph.D.

Dr. Richard E. Rogala was a nationally-recognized consultant to management. He received his B.A. and M.A. from DePaul University and his doctorate in psychology from the Illinois Institute of Psychology.

He began his career as an assistant professor at Lewis University in Lockport, Illinois. He was then appointed Chairman of the Department of Psychology at Lewis and subsequently was named Director of Institutional Research and Assistant to the President of Lewis University.

Dr. Rogala worked for eighteen years with a firm of psychologists as a Consultant to Management; the last five years he served as president of the organization. In 1986, he started the firm that is now known as Rogala and Orr.

During a professional career that spanned over thirty years, Dr. Rogala conducted management assessments, coached and counseled managers and leaders of America's leading companies, and worked with groups to help develop managers.

He was a member of the American Psychological Association, the Illinois Psychological Association, and The Greater Chicago Association of Industrial/Organizational Psychologists.

Dr. Rogala was published in many trade journals and magazines, including Industry Week, Business Today, Supervision Magazine, Hospital Purchasing News, American Salesman and Ackerman Warehousing Forum.

Richard E. Rogala, Jr.

Rick Rogala is an expert on success and achievement. As an award winning business executive, he served as general manager of five different television stations, and is the only general manager to have built three new television facilities, two from the ground up. In a broadcast career spanning twenty-two years, Rick Rogala worked with teams at his stations to harness their full potential and exceed customer expectations, creating growth and success.

As a speaker, author, radio personality and consultant, Rick Rogala empowers people and organizations to achieve the extraordinary. He developed the trademarked FUEL system (Focus, Urgency, Enthusiasm and Leadership) for achievement based upon his life experiences, twenty-two years of success in business, and the philosophy of his father, Richard E Rogala, Ph.D. who was a psychologist and coach to captains of industry.

Rick Rogala is President of Rogala and Associates, a firm of specialists in growth strategies, communication, motivation, personal performance and organizational achievement. Rick and his family live in Carmel, Indiana.

Harness the incredible power of FUEL!

Rick Rogala will empower you to achieve the extraordinary by harnessing the power of FUEL in your business and life!

Find out how he can engage your organization to create a breakthrough right away. Write to Rick at rick@rickrogala.com to start a conversation that will change what you expect from yourself forever.

Rick is an expert on success and achievement. As an award-winning business executive, speaker, author, radio personality, trainer and consultant, he works with businesses and teams to capitalize on their full potential and exceed customer expectations, creating growth and success.

Rick leads dynamic presentations in the context of the new order of business in America.

Leadership
Growth Strategies
Positive Communication
Motivation
Sales
Marketing
Organizational Achievement
Managing Change
Business, Media and Marketing

Contact Rick at rick@rickrogala.com or visit www.rickrogala.com.

www.ingramcontent.com/pod-product-compliance
Lightning Source LLC
Chambersburg PA
CBHW030355290526
45785CB00004B/1764